Teen Law
A Practical Legal Guide for
Teenagers Everywhere

(Not a substitute for legal advice or legal represent~

David Levin

Vandeplas Publishing

United States of America

Teen law: a practical legal guide for teenagers everywhere

Levin, David

David Levin is a member of the State Bar of Texas and practices law in Houston

Published by:

Vandeplas Publishing - November 2009

801 International Parkway, 5th Floor
Lake Mary, FL. 32746
USA

www.vandeplaspublishing.com

ISBN: 978-1-60042-087-0

Dedication

Teen Law is dedicated to Peggy Levin, whose vision and inspiration are its soul.

DISCLAIMERS

Legal Disclaimer

This book is not a substitute for legal advice or legal representation, which should be sought only from a licensed attorney in the state where the legal matter arose. Legal advice and legal representation are based on an attorney/client relationship, rather than a book. This work is of a general informational nature only. It may or may not be correct with respect to a particular matter. It is not intended as legal representation or legal advice.

Investment Disclaimer

There is information in this book relating to investing. This information is not intended as investment advice, which should be sought only from a licensed investment professional. The material in this book is intended only to give the teenage reader a general, basic understanding of the subject matter, rather than specific investment guidance.

No Endorsement

No person, institution, or company endorses this book or its contents.

TABLE OF CONTENTS

CHAPTER 1 — Why does the law matter to me, a teenager? (The importance of following the law)

There was a man who had lived his life as he saw fit, an independent and tough man, traveling around on his motorcycle, finding adventure and fun where he could, not tied down by the normal relationships of life. On one of his trips, he went to a beach community, where he met a young woman and had a fight with another man over her. He had been in fights before, usually winning them because of his military hand-to-hand training. But this time, things took a different turn. He hurt the other man badly, and the injured fellow filed aggravated assault charges, carrying punishment including jail time. The man was brought to trial and exhibited an arrogant, defiant attitude toward the charge. As the evidence against him mounted, the man's attitude changed. Seeing his freedom slipping away, the man began to show fear as he pleaded for his attorney to help him stay out of prison. (This is a true story from a case known to the author.)

The law is serious business. It can make and break people and companies. It can be a strong ally of those who understand it, and it can crush those who do not. You may be aware that in recent history of the United States the law was used to elect a president and it was also used to bring down a sitting president. Many very able people argue the law with great, persuasive skill, some for the prosecution and some for the defense. These people are aggressive and smart and love a legal fight. In fact, of all the professions that have come and gone over the years, of all that have been important from time to time, of all that have been powerful over the years, one profession has remained at the top—the legal profession. Many of the most powerful and wealthy people in America are members of this profession, and many of our most influential leaders have been lawyers, including some of our nation's presidents. Additionally, for sheer economic potential, no other profession can match the legal profession, not medicine or dentistry or accounting or even business. That, at least in part, is why such able people become lawyers.

Why do you suppose that these facts are true? Probably the single best answer is that developed nations, such as the United States, must rely on a set of laws to maintain order so that the nation can remain developed. In spite of all of the flaws in the legal system, it is the basis of our growth and development. Think about it for a minute. If there were no laws regulating the drug industry, would you feel confident taking hyped medicines that may or may not be safe? If we had no aviation laws, do you think that our airline industry would be as safe as it is today? The safety records of those industries are directly based on the laws that regulate them and protect the public. All of our modern laws are derived from the way that our nation began. For, while certain nations were ruled by kings and queens, some of whom were good rulers while others were not, our nation was established upon a set of laws designed to insure that people would be free while reasonably governed in an orderly society. That is why you may have heard it said that we are a nation of laws, rather than a nation of men.

So, now you understand that the tradition of relying on laws is a very strong one in the United States. Hopefully, you also realize that it is equally important for you to respect and follow those laws. However, if you aren't convinced and ask, "Why? I'm a teenager with lots of other important stuff to think about. Like dressing cool. And being accepted by the other kids, you know, the ones that count. And having fun. And, you know, all the neat teenage stuff," then think about these facts:

1. Did you realize that a criminal record can dog you for your entire life? You may be required to disclose such a record when you apply to college or to graduate or professional school. For example, look at a typical law school application. It requires the full

disclosure of all criminal charges and cases involving the applicant, except for minor traffic matters. DWIs are not minor traffic charges. They are serious criminal matters which must be disclosed. And some jobs, such as those in the government and in certain high tech industries, also require similar disclosure. Don't think that a juvenile record can be hidden from everyone who might want to know about your past. While it is true that a juvenile record, meaning one that came into existence while a person was young, most often younger than 16, is "sealed," that record can still be examined for certain special reasons, such as when you apply to law school.

2. If you commit a serious crime as a juvenile, you can be certified as an adult to stand trial, meaning that the adult range of punishment can be applied if you are found guilty.

3. If you break the law while you are a juvenile and hurt someone, your parents can be held responsible and required to pay the other person's damages (there goes your college fund).

4. After you pass the juvenile age your record from then on becomes an open book for anyone who may care to look, such as every potential employer who may do a background check. In fact, laws covering some jobs, such as truck drivers, require that the employer check to make sure the applicant is safe for that particular job. Would you like some guy with several

DWIs to drive a gasoline tanker truck on roads you use? Today, the law imposes duties on employers to check the criminal backgrounds of their applicants to weed out people who are dangerous, such as those with a history of violence.

5. Should you hurt someone and the other person sues you and wins the case and you don't pay that person, then you owe him or her a debt until you do pay. That debt can wreck your credit for years to come, preventing you from buying things on credit, like a car.

6. The cost to hire a good lawyer to defend you against a criminal charge can be staggering. It is nothing for a top criminal lawyer to ask for a $25,000 retainer and to submit a final bill of $100,000 or more. Yet, parents of a child whose future is riding on the outcome of a criminal case will mortgage everything they own to find that money, even if it takes a lifetime to pay it back.

7. Some criminal charges, like DWI, involve several types of punishment, such as jail time, fines, community service, mandatory counseling or alcohol classes, and loss of your driver's license. That means that if you drive to a job or to school or to guitar lessons after school, guess what—your life is about to change for the worse. Look at Appendix One for a summary of one state's criminal laws and the applicable punishments.

8. Legal proceedings are public, open to the press and the curious. People are not tried for criminal charges in secret. That means that you and your family are subject to the ridicule of others, which can be devastating, even if unfair.

9. Lastly, be aware that a juvenile charged with a felony must give a DNA sample for a government database, meaning that person loses some privacy.

Hopefully, now it is a little clearer why teenagers need to know something about the law. That is the reason for this book. No book can give you the detailed legal advice that a lawyer can provide, and we do not intend to give you legal advice here. Rather, if we can open your mind to see some legal problems before they fall on you, then, maybe you can avoid them and live a happier life. If you want to broaden your knowledge and begin your pre-adult life in a better way, read on.

CHAPTER 2—Torts anyone? (Injuries and damages to others)

If someone should offer you a "tort," run as fast as you can. They aren't talking about something good to eat. A tort is a legal concept. Basically, it is a legal wrong committed by someone against another person, causing some loss or damage for which the first person is responsible. The law says that the other person can recover money damages for the wrong done to him. Who pays the bill? You guessed it—you, or your parents, if you committed the tort as a minor. If you can't pay the money, then you owe a debt to that other person, a debt that gets bigger and bigger as time goes on from the accrual of interest. So what can be the basis of a tort? A car accident, a fight, a stupid prank, or a false and hurtful public comment can be the basis of a tort.

Suppose you are driving the family car with your friends, having a great time, going a little over the speed limit, and, wham, you run into the car in front of you. Look out! You have just committed a tort. The lady in the other car can now sue you, and maybe your parents, for her injuries and car damages. Her bill can get pretty big: pain and suffering from her whiplash, medical damages to treat her now and in the future, her future pain and suffering, her present and future impairment (such as from her neck becoming stiff), her lost wages when she can't work while she gets better, the cost to fix her car, the cost to rent a car while her car is being fixed, interest on that total bill, and other things as well (like court costs, which can get high). You and your parents now have a big problem, aside from them being mad at you. Oh sure, your family might have insurance, but that can't take care of everything. For example, your insurance policy may have a deductible, meaning an amount of the total bill that your parents will have to pay out of their own pockets. Even if your family has insurance you may still face a lawsuit, which will take up your time and energy. When it comes time to renew the insurance policy, the cost of the new policy probably will be much greater. Also, it's possible that the insurance company will cancel the policy or refuse to renew it, meaning that your parents will be forced to find a new policy, usually at higher cost. If the accident is a serious one, criminal charges can be filed, which the insurance policy can't fix. So, what is the moral of this story? Be careful in the car. Accidents can cost your family money, cause you and your parents sleepless nights, and change your life forever. Your car instantly can become a dangerous machine. Treat it like that at all times.

Let's suppose that you are a good driver, but a little hot tempered, particularly when it comes to your manhood (assuming of course that you are a guy, especially trying to impress the ladies). Some punk comes up to your girlfriend in school and teases her about her sweater, and you knock him silly. That's different from the car wreck, right? Well, the correct answer is, "Yes and no." It's still a tort, but a different kind. Because you assaulted someone, you have committed an intentional tort, meaning that you did it on purpose. The poor guy lying on the ground with his teeth beside him on the floor can sue you for his damages (the cost to fix his teeth, psychological counseling, lost wages from his waiter's job, etc.). But he can also sue you for something else: "punitive damages," meaning extra money to punish you and prevent you from slugging someone in the future. In the case of intentional torts, most likely your family has no insurance to pay. Most insurance policies do not pay for damages from intentional torts. What is the result? Well, aside from the possible criminal charge for assault, the other guy and his parents can sue you and your parents for damages and try to collect them (there goes your college fund again). If you don't have the money to pay, then the amount you owe follows you as an ever increasing debt until you do pay, hurting your credit all that time. What is the moral here? Control your temper and don't do stupid things. Act like a responsible adult. It's better to walk away than to harm your future over something that means little or nothing. Knowing when to "fold 'em" is worth a lot. This is especially true of road rage. Even if you win a road rage incident, you lose. The reason is that road rage can result in your being sued for an intentional tort and prosecuted for a crime. Calm down behind the wheel. Let the other guy pass you, and don't salute him with your middle finger. Be smart. Besides, that other guy may be crazy (and have a gun to end your life—it's happening more and more today).

Now what is the story about this tort based on a person saying something false and hurtful about someone else? The law provides that it is wrong to say or write publicly something false that hurts another person. This kind of activity is called a "defamation," and can lead to a lawsuit. Suppose you say that Joe stole something from his employer or that Sally is loose with all the boys or that Sam's father physically abuses Sam. If these statements are false, look out, they can be the basis of a suit against you. Joe can sue you for his lost wages if his employer fired him; Sally can sue you for her mental anguish; Sam's father can sue you for his mental anguish and psychological counseling if his mind gets messed up from public ridicule. Also, just like the intentional tort, your family may not have insurance to cover this kind of wrong, meaning you will face a lawsuit without anyone to pay your lawyer's fee or the final judgment amount you will owe. The lesson here is simple: don't start or spread rumors, orally, in writing or by email, that can hurt others. It's better to be a listener and not a talker where hurtful gossip is concerned.

These examples aren't all of the situations that can be the basis of a tort. They are only a few of the ways you can get in trouble. Remember the Golden Rule: if you mess with someone else, he might take your gold. So, stop and think before you act, and, most probably, you'll save yourself and your family a lot of grief.

We are not through with this subject, because we have yet to explain the criminal side of certain types of illegal behavior, like car wrecks. Did you know that each year almost 15,000 people die in speeding car crashes? Every one of those deaths represents an opportunity for the district attorney to charge someone with a criminal offense. You understand that a criminal charge is not a tort? A criminal charge is different—it represents the state charging a person with a serious violation of the law for which a fine and jail time can be assessed.

In the event of a car crash resulting in a death, the person speeding or driving recklessly or losing control of the car or running the red light can be charged with a criminal offense. Such an offense can be negligent homicide, manslaughter or even murder, depending on the severity of the facts (someone doing 100 through a school zone is considered to be doing very reckless, criminal driving). These charges can be felonies, the most serious class of criminal charge. You see, your car is a potential weapon that can kill. A teenager who kills another person with a car can be certified as an adult, to stand trial before a jury and suffer the punishment of an adult, if found guilty. This is not a juvenile court matter, but, rather, a full-blown criminal court trial that many times makes the news.

These same criminal laws apply to other means of conveyance, such as boats, snowmobiles, and planes.

Operate them with caution for the harm they can cause. Each year people die in accidents involving these machines.

Slow down and drive carefully. You do not want to be a murderer, living with that guilt for your entire life and, possibly, the stain of having been convicted of a terrible crime.

Chapter 3—You mean school has laws too? (School law)

Now you have learned about torts, and you're feeling pretty good, thinking that you are going to walk the straight and narrow and avoid those land mines. But wait a minute, what about all those school rules? Do you need to learn about them also? You had better, because they're just as important as the other laws.

All states have education laws, bodies of rules regulating a state's educational system. Some of these rules relate directly to the conduct of the students. And some misinformed people believe that the student is untouchable because he or she is shielded by laws protecting minors or by other laws guaranteeing a person's civil rights ("trial by jury" or the "right to a lawyer" for example). A student doesn't lose his or her basic civil rights, but those rights are handled a little differently when it comes to the educational process. Our lawmakers realize that school officials must be given certain rights in dealing with students to keep the schools orderly and safe and to educate large groups of kids. Otherwise, the school system wouldn't work. The educational laws allow school officials to impose their rules before they get into any heavy duty legal proceedings. Basically, here's what happens. School districts establish rules dealing with student conduct. These rules provide that the school officials can handle problems themselves, within reason. If a student breaks the rules, like cheating or fighting, then a school official, such as the principal, can correct the situation according to the established rule for that kind of misconduct.

So what happens if a student breaks the rules? Can he sue if he doesn't like the punishment he receives? The simple answers are: first, he will be subject to the punishment that the school officials prescribe, such as detention; and, second, from a practical point he can't sue right away, at least not until the school administrative disciplinary process is over. Most state educational laws provide two to three levels of student punishment. The first is for minor student offenses, such as getting into a shoving match with a student, being disrespectful to a teacher, causing a minor disturbance, etc. The second is for more serious offenses, often those disrupting the educational process, such as yelling at a teacher or getting into a fight. The third and most serious category involves violations that put the safety of others at risk, such as bringing a weapon to school or making a terrorist threat. The thing to remember in this area of the law is that the school officials have already thought of how to deal with different types of student misconduct and have decided the means of correcting the situations. Minor problems will normally be addressed by some type of in-school punishment, like detention. Severe types of misconduct will be addressed by placing the student in an alternative school, some place with strict rules and few privileges (no football or cheerleading here). Dangerous or repeated misconduct will be handled by expulsion, meaning you are kicked out of school for a period of time, maybe even the rest of the current term and the entire next term.

You also need to understand that most schools' behavior rules apply not only on school property but also to school activities on adjacent property (like the road next to the school; for example, alcohol in your car parked on the street next to the school will be covered by school rules against alcohol). Those same rules also apply to school trips (like basketball tournaments in another city) and school activities at remote locations (the school bonfire on some ranch in the sticks).

Let's say that you fall into that unfortunate category three, the real bad one, and the school wants to punish you severely. What can you expect and what can you do about it? We are going to assume that the punishment is the problem, that you can't accept being expelled (expulsion is really rough because it can mean the loss of some of your credits and difficulty getting into any other public school while you are expelled from your school). The first thing you need to do is ask for a copy of the school rules that relate to your situation. Second, read them. You will probably note that you are entitled to a hearing, which you will want to request. But those hearings don't usually change the principal's decision to punish you. The school rules provide for such hearings to comply with the constitutional requirement to give the student due process. The judge at such a hearing is usually some lawyer selected and paid by the school. So, guess with whom he is normally going to side? You guessed it—the school official who hammered you. However, the hearing can be helpful because it will allow you to hear the school's case against you and give you some chance of changing the punishment decision, even if it isn't a good chance.

It is also important to remember to do everything in writing, such as requesting the hearing, and to do it within the time limits in the rules. After the hearing, which you most likely will lose, you'll get your best chance to change the punishment decision—a hearing before the school board. Remember, the punishment decision was probably made by some principal or assistant principal and confirmed by a school administrator, all of whom are employees of the school district who support each other, kind of like family members. Many of them want only to get rid of a problem (you) rather than dealing with it. That's why it's hard to get the decision of one of those people reversed or lessened by his buddy. The school board is different; its members aren't part of the school good old boy system. The school board members are moms and dads who are elected as volunteers to oversee the school officials. Your pleas for leniency will be better received by the school board than the school officials, especially if you take your parents with you and all of you say you are sorry and will behave in the future. Chances are the school board will hear you and reduce your punishment to something you can live with. But remember: BE POLITE AND SORRY FOR YOUR WRONGDOING before the school board. Arrogance there will do you little good.

You are probably wondering whether or not you will need a lawyer up to this point in the proceedings to overturn or lessen that punishment decision you feel is unfair. The answer is, "Most likely not." The proceedings through the school board are very informal and don't require a lawyer. In fact, a lawyer may even hurt your chances during these proceedings, mainly because having a lawyer many times complicates matters and paints you as trying to get off on a legal technicality. Save the lawyer for the next step, if necessary— the suit you file to overturn the bad decision that the school board wouldn't overturn or lessen. That's when you bring out that hired gun to look for the legal technicality.

Now, let's turn to the age old problem of the student, and his or her parents, who are very unhappy with an extracurricular activity decision: you know, who was selected as the starting quarterback or elected to be head cheerleader or made the starting five on the basketball team (of course, those chosen ones are other kids, and you think they were unfairly selected over you and want to sue). Here's the straight and skinny in this area: your chances of winning one of these cases are almost zero. The reason is because the courts prefer to let the school officials handle school matters, especially those involving extracurricular activities. If you choose to sue to overturn one of these results, GOOD LUCK. You will need it because you and your parents probably will spend a lot of money and run out of time (meaning you will graduate before the appeals are over) and still lose. What is the moral here? Do your best and have some confidence that the coach wants to field the best team or the cheerleader sponsor wants the snappiest squad. The truth is that their careers depend on the coaches producing the best teams possible.

There is another minefield to discuss in this area of school law. Many times when a student is involved in some behavior problem, the school officials will call the police and seek to charge the student with a crime. Take, for example, the student who hits another student. The hitter can be charged with assault. Similarly, students have been charged with theft, making terror threats, possessing illegal drugs or weapons, arson, and other crimes. Exercise self-control before you do something that can be classified as a breach of a school rule <u>and</u> a crime, such as fighting. By the way, sharing your prescription drug with a fellow student, even for the sole reason of helping the other student, is an expulsion offense under many schools' "zero tolerance" drug rules and a criminal offense under states' drug laws. Don't try to help your friends this way. Be savvy and send your friend to the school nurse. That way he/she gets the right help and you don't get the shaft.

We leave school law with a look at "truancy" law, which requires all people under a certain age, sixteen or seventeen in most states, to attend school. If you are absent from school a lot, without a good excuse, you and your parents can be arrested and brought before a court for punishment. Why do schools care whether you attend classes? Schools receive state tax money for each day students are there, but not when they aren't. Get it?

There is a state law matter related to school, and, while not a behavior rule, you should know about it. In most states, if you report personal abuse to your teacher or school counselor, he/she is required by law to alert the authorities, such as child welfare and/or police. If you are being abused, keep this law in mind; it could save your life. However, if you get mad at your dad just because he won't let you go to the football game, do not lie to your teacher and tell her your dad is an abuser. Such a lie could land him in jail, require him to hire a lawyer, expose him to public ridicule and hatred, and subject you to prosecution for making a false statement.

As to false statements to police, know that it is a crime, and a felony in some states, for a person to file a false government report. Trained police interrogators will question you about any suspicious reports, eventually get the truth, and arrest you when you admit, "I lied to the police about that coach; he really didn't hit me; I was just mad at him; I'm sorry!"

The cops love to arrest such teens at school to make the point to the other kids that a false police report is a crime. It's very embarrassing when they slap the cuffs on a student in the cafeteria and take him away.

In this country, education can lead to a good life. You don't need to be born rich. Statistics show more education leads to more income and a greater chance of keeping your job in a tough economy, when the less educated are being laid off.

Here is a real life scenario: mixed-race kid comes from a broken home; moves from school to school; is raised by his grandparents; is a good athlete and spends time on the basketball court, maybe a little too much; admits using drugs; lets his grades slip for a while; gets back on track with his studies and makes good grades; gets into a good university; completes his college education and earns a professional degree; know what they call him today? "Mr. President." *Comprende*? Don't blow your school opportunity; it can take you a very long way.

CHAPTER 4 — Sex could be hazardous to your future. (Laws relating to teen sex)

Sex is big business these days. It sells magazines, movies, songs, clothes, and other things. It's hyped by people who make vast sums from a misguided public who are persuaded that casual sex is exciting by some actor pretending that it is. The truth is that sex is great, in the right context, but it can be devastating in the wrong one. We want you to understand the difference between reality and hype. It's a big deal.

Let's assume that you and your boyfriend/girlfriend have underage sex, meaning when you are younger than eighteen. What can happen, from a legal standpoint that is?

There are civil implications and criminal implications. Let's look at some of the more likely ones.

Civil implications involve the civil laws, those laws dealing with contracts or torts or employment matters or domestic relations, which is the area where sexual activity falls. In our situation, where you and your boyfriend/girlfriend have underage sex, one obvious result is that you might produce a baby. If you do, remember that you, as a parent, have the obligation to support that child until he/she becomes an adult (eighteen). That means that you can be ordered by a court to pay money toward the child's support for many years. This court order can be enforced with the garnishment of your wages, which is when your employer is required to pay part of your wages to a state agency which will then pay that money, each month, to the custodial parent of the child.

You should also be aware that all of the states have laws making it a crime to avoid paying child support. Most often, if the state can prove you willingly or knowingly avoided a child support obligation, you can be prosecuted for this crime (a fine and jail time are possible). The federal laws also include a similar statute, which applies if you are in one state and your child is in another.

Let us assume that you are the pregnant girl who decides to correct this situation by merely obtaining an abortion. You have heard that the Supreme Court has given the woman the sole right to terminate the pregnancy. You have a simple solution, right? Well, maybe it's not quite that simple. Keep in mind that you are a teenager. If you are under eighteen, you might have to notify your parents and get their approval before you have the abortion. You see, thirty-four states have laws requiring that a person under eighteen notify and/or obtain the permission of one or both parents before getting an abortion. Your doctor will know the law, because it affects him or her too.

But there's more to tell you about sex and our civil laws. Let's assume that after the sex is over, your boyfriend/girlfriend has a change of heart and claims that the sex was not consensual (the other person says he/she didn't want to have sex but was forced to do so—or became drunk or high and was taken advantage of while out of it). You and your parents could be sued by that other person and his/her parents for damages, just as in the tort situation. What could those damages be? They could include money for an assault, pain and suffering, mental anguish, future psychological problems, medical bills, and psychological counseling costs. The total bill could be staggering, and the psychological impact of the legal proceedings on you and your family probably will be equally adverse.

Now that we have looked at the civil side of sex, let's turn our attention to the criminal laws, which would include the laws that put people in jail or fine them for conduct regarded as so bad that society must punish the person who did it. In the situation described above, if the other person complains that the sex wasn't consensual or that he or she was underage, you could be charged with criminal assault, injury to a child, rape, or statutory rape. Assault can be merely an unwanted touching. However, generally accepted social gestures, such as handshakes and pats-on-the-back, are exceptions. Rape is forcing yourself sexually on another. Injury to a child is any harmful conduct to a minor. Statutory rape is sex with a person younger than a certain age, such as sixteen, even if the sex was consensual (the idea here is that persons under a certain age cannot give fully informed consent to have sex). Statutory rape laws exist in all states, and the forbidden age for sex varies from fourteen to eighteen with more than half of the states setting that age at sixteen.

All of these activities can be crimes with severe punishments ranging from fines to jail time, and they apply to males and females alike. You can see that in our situation you could find yourself in the unfortunate position of being charged with criminal violations just for engaging in a moment of passion with the wrong person. And consider this fact: the criminal laws covering sex crimes are expanding to cover more activities, especially when it comes to minors. For example, it is illegal to look into a place where privacy is expected, like a bathroom, (the "Peeping Tom" law) or to pull a girl's pants down in public (sexual assault). If you are convicted of a sex crime, especially with a minor, you may be required to register as a sex offender for life and be unable to get certain jobs, such as a teacher. Registered sex offenders can also be restricted in where they live (not too close to schools, etc.).

The moral of this lesson is that sex can create serious consequences and should be reserved for a time in your life when you are ready and able to deal with those consequences. Remember this also: you should take great care to make sure that the other person is ready and willing to deal with the sexual encounter. If he or she is not, you could end up getting hurt very badly.

CHAPTER 5—You mean I can't drink alcohol either? (Laws relating to teen consumption of alcohol)

Until you're twenty-one you can't drink alcohol, at least if you want to avoid some nasty legal problems. Alcohol, like sex, is hyped by people who make a lot of money from it. Truthfully, there's nothing wrong with alcohol, so long as it's handled correctly. But there's the problem. Our government leaders have concluded that young people, more often than not, can't handle alcohol until they are older. That's the basis of underage drinking laws. So let's explore some of those laws and how they can affect you.

Assume that you are under twenty-one and drink some beer. You're having a great time, but an undercover police officer observes you drinking at the party. Then he sees you and your friends leave the party and laugh all the way to the parking lot, before you get in your car and drive everybody to the lake for more beer. Sounds great, right? Wrong! You are in a world of legal trouble that can cost you a lot.

First of all, under a state's Zero Tolerance law any detectable amount of alcohol in your system is illegal. According to this law, if you are driving and your blood alcohol level is very small, not up to the drunk level, you can still be charged with DUI, driving under the influence. And if, unfortunately, your blood alcohol reading reaches the level of impairment, in many states .08, then the charge is DWI, driving while intoxicated, which is more severe. But the police aren't finished: they can also charge you with the separate criminal offenses of "open alcohol container in a vehicle," "minor in possession" and "public intoxication," each of which carries its own punishment. Now, let's suppose that you didn't drive the car at all. What can the police charge you with? The answer is: everything except DWI and DUI. You see, it's illegal for a person under twenty-one to buy, consume, possess, or lie about his or her age to get alcohol, even if he or she doesn't drive with alcohol in his or her system (see Appendix One).

A special word is in order about driving while intoxicated. The public is outraged by the increasing number of DWI injuries and deaths. This outrage has caused our lawmakers to increase the punishment under our DWI laws. Therefore, understand that DWI is not a traffic offense; it's a serious criminal offense. In fact, repeated DWIs or a DWI that hurts or kills someone or one with a minor in the car can be a felony, the most serious criminal charge. If convicted of a felony, you can go to jail, lose your right to vote, and be tagged with the horrible label "felon." Don't start your life that way.

You may be wondering what punishments can be assessed for alcohol offenses by minors. Here is what could happen to you: driver's license suspension for up to a year or more (it costs to get it back after the suspension), a fine up to several thousands of dollars, jail time up to a year or more, a number of hours of community service, other costs that you must pay, such as costs of testing your blood for alcohol when you are on probation.

Now, you might say that if a policeman stops you while driving, you will just refuse any breath test and avoid a charge. Think again. The lawmakers have already thought about people doing that. Here's what can happen. First, the law automatically suspends the driver's license of anyone who refuses an alcohol test. Second, the fact that you refused the test may be used against you as evidence at trial (so the jury will automatically become suspicious). Third, the police officer will most likely say that he or she observed your car weaving or speeding or moving erratically and that you stammered or slurred your speech, had glazed eyes, couldn't walk a straight line, smelled like alcohol, and, in the opinion of the officer, acted like a drunk. Guess what? You lose. The jury will believe the officer and convict you.

There are proper ways to handle an alcohol charge as a part of your defense. Let's stress that different lawyers have different strategies for handling DWI and DUI cases. If you refuse the officer's request to take an alcohol test, then there is no alcohol test evidence to use against you at trial, which makes the state's case a little harder. However, remember the practical points made above for refusing the test. If you agree to take the alcohol test, probably a breath test, it might not register enough alcohol to charge you, especially if some time has elapsed since you drank the alcohol. Also, the prosecutor will not be able to say you refused the test. In either case, be polite and do not admit to being drunk. Say that you would like to get a lawyer before you say anything to the police or sign a confession. If the charge is anything other than DUI or DWI, you can ask the judge to place you on "deferred adjudication," meaning probation, at the end of which—if you have been good—the judge will dismiss the charge. But even with the dismissal, you may be required to disclose the charge on a school or employment application. If you are charged with the more serious DUI or DWI (they are more serious because someone could have been killed), deferred adjudication isn't usually possible under the law. However, there are still things you can do to defend yourself. You will likely need an experienced DWI criminal lawyer. Your lawyer will probably look into the following: can the police prove you were behind the wheel? (if not, the DWI or DUI charge won't stick); did the police properly calibrate the test machine and was the operator trained to operate it? (if not, the results can be challenged as inaccurate); was the stop of the car legal in the first place, meaning did the officer have probable cause to think a crime had been or was being committed or that evidence of a crime existed or cause to be reasonably suspicious of criminal activity? (if not, all of the evidence obtained by the officer, including the alcohol test result, can't be used). If your lawyer can weaken the evidence against you by any of these methods, then he or she may be able to negotiate a deal that will let you receive a lesser charge, such as MIP, minor in possession, which can be handled by deferred adjudication, explained below, or, in some very lucky cases, dismissal with only a slap on the wrist, such as your completion of an alcohol class.

You should also know that DWI/DUI laws apply to operating boats, planes and certain kinds of machinery. That is, the law makes it illegal to be impaired or affected by alcohol while driving any of those machines. Don't be fooled to believe that you are completely free of the police on the waters of a lake or a bay or a river. The police patrol those areas in boats, looking for erratic boat movement, ready to pull you over to take a breath test and arrest you if it shows a reading at or above the intoxication level. One special point about boats is this: generally, it's illegal for children to be in a boat on the water without life preservers on. There's the probable cause to stop your boat and search.

There is a new development in this area of the law: a statute allowing police to involuntarily take a blood sample under certain conditions, such as your refusing a breath test and a child being in the vehicle when stopped. Such a law makes it tougher to escape DWI/DUI detection and punishment, another good reason to avoid this land mine.

Before leaving this subject, we should note two similar legal matters. First, it is illegal to buy, use, or possess tobacco/snuff if you are under eighteen. Second, it is a crime to possess a fake ID. Police officers have been known to be undercover at quick marts, waiting for some baby-faced kid to present an ID saying he or she is twenty-one. "Sure you are!" the cop says as he puts the cuffs on the minor.

The moral of this chapter is not to teach you how to escape punishment. Rather, it is to help you avoid the problem in the first place. Do you see what a royal hassle all this legal stuff is? Use good judgment and wait to drink alcohol until you are of an age to handle it. Our lawmakers have spent many years thinking about what that age should be. Listen to them and follow what they say. After all, they're doing all of this for your future and the futures of others they will never know.

CHAPTER 6—It's okay, I have a prescription!
(Laws relating to teen consumption of illegal drugs)

We are going to presume that you know that use of hard core drugs, like cocaine, meth, heroine, etc., is squarely against the law and can get you in big trouble. If you know this, then you also know that possessing, passing, buying, selling, or transporting controlled substances, without legal authority, is illegal under state and federal law, carrying severe penalties. In this vein, be aware that a few states allow marijuana use for medicinal purposes, if the user has a prescription. However, the rub here is that federal law does not agree, making possession or use of marijuana a crime. Since federal law trumps state law, if you are in one of those states, the feds can still arrest you, and sometimes do, and charge you with a crime. Therefore, don't let your buddy say, "It's okay. We're in a state where marijuana is legal. Let's have some fun." It's likely federal agents are watching.

There are other drug-related things you may not know, and we'll try to cover some of them here. For example, you may not know that the law contains what are called "minimum sentencing guidelines" for criminal offenses, which means that judges are expected by our lawmakers to be tough on drug offenders—you know, such as giving jail time for certain violations of the law, even if you plead guilty (see Appendix One). Did you also know the misuse of a legally obtained prescription drug is illegal, such as when a person uses another's prescription or when someone takes too much of his own drug or processes it into some other drug to get high? And what is the law concerning paint and glue being inhaled for a drug high? You guessed it: that's also against the law.

Do you think that our laws are tough? Well, you had better be very careful if you travel in other countries, because many of them are much tougher on drug law violators. Be aware that most other countries don't give you the legal protections that the United States does, like a right to an attorney. In fact, some of those other laws provide the death penalty for certain drug offenses. What are we trying to tell you here? Be especially careful if you travel internationally. Don't take illegal drugs with you; don't hold some other person's drugs; don't transport the drugs of another person; don't possess, hold or transport any unknown package for anyone.

Now, do you remember the chapter about school law? Well know this about drugs and school law: the sale, consumption, possession, use, or being under the influence of illegal drugs on school property or during a school event, on or off school property, or on adjacent property to the school can be one of those very serious school offenses that can get you in real trouble with the school officials (and the police, who use drug dogs). Don't do any of those things. They are among the worst choices you can make.

Answer this scenario: you and a friend are having a great time smoking weed while driving the local strip and ogling the women. A cop stops you for not wearing your seat belts, before discovering a large bag of weed in your car. The cop arrests you both and laughs, saying, "Man, it's going to be a shame when we sell this fine sports car and keep the money." You gasp. "What do you mean? This is my car." The officer looks at you with a smile. "Not anymore. You just gave it to the government." The question: Is the police officer right? Answer: "Yes." Reason: The law provides that property involved in illegal drug activity can be confiscated and sold, with the proceeds going to the government to help pay for the fight against illegal drugs.

Also, be aware that in most states it is illegal to possess drug paraphernalia (you know, the things people use to put illegal drugs into their bodies, like heroine needles and hashish pipes and cocaine straws). Don't think you can just tell the police officer that those items are being used for proper purposes. The officer will have them tested at a lab, and even small amounts of drug residue will be detected, resulting in additional drug charges.

We refer you to the end of Appendix One for descriptions of some Texas drug crimes and their punishments. However, this is not an exhaustive list, and may not be accurate in your state. But here's a good rule to follow: if the substance you are considering can kill you, mess up your mind, make you high, impair your normal abilities, or upset your mother, stay away from it, no matter what some other kid says.

Before we close this chapter, let us leave you with a final thought. Did you know that certain illegal drugs can alter your mind? This isn't hype; it's fact. Drug users can experience different types of mental illness from using illegal drugs. Now, here's the legal part: a person who is found by a judge to be mentally ill and a danger to himself or to others can be involuntarily committed to a mental hospital for a specified amount of time. These places resemble jails, with bars and locked steel doors. The atmosphere is grim. Illegal drugs can put you in such a place—again and again and again, for the rest of your life. Do you understand the moral of this chapter? We sincerely hope so. It is one of the most important morals you will ever hear.

CHAPTER 7 — How many tickets before I can't drive anymore? (Traffic/Curfew laws)

This chapter deals with traffic and curfew violations. They just seem to go hand in hand, maybe because you normally will have driven to the place where you're not supposed to be at that hour of the night.

Let's start by answering the question in the title of this chapter. How many tickets does it take, anyway? The number varies from state to state. But, under one state's law, the number is four moving violations in a year. Moving violations include: speeding, running a red light, running a stop sign, failure to yield right of way to someone else, failure to control your speed, and changing lanes in an unsafe manner. Nonmoving violations include such things as parking meter, no parking zone, and equipment (like a dead headlight or taillight) offenses. Nonmoving violations usually don't affect your driver's license, but they can cause you to be arrested if you ignore them, meaning you don't get them dismissed or pay them—such as when you just put them in your glove box, hoping somehow they will go away, which doesn't work because the police keep copies and will come looking for you if you don't take care of them.

What other kinds of traffic violations are there? Some of the more common ones are: failure to wear your seatbelt, failure to properly display your registration or safety sticker, failure to carry proof of financial responsibility (auto liability insurance), and failure to wear your glasses if your driver's license requires that you do so. A conviction for failure to wear your glasses can, in some states, result in losing your driver's license. And, no, driver's education can't excuse such an offense. Take it very seriously.

If you should lose your driver's license by order of a court (or fail to renew it) and you drive while your license is suspended, you've not committed a traffic violation. Rather, you have committed a criminal violation for which a fine and jail time can be assessed as the punishment. Similarly, just as we told you about DWI and DUI, driving without a valid license (it expired and wasn't renewed) is a criminal offense rather than a traffic violation. Avoid these charges!

You should also understand that most states require that you have auto liability insurance and all banks which loan money to buy a car require that you also have auto loss insurance covering that car. So, it's important you understand that your parents must have auto insurance for you and the car you drive. If you get those moving tickets we talked about or if you get a DWI or a DUI or if you damage your car more than the insurance company likes, the insurance company can cancel your parents' auto policy or refuse to renew it when it ends. This places your parents in the difficult position of having to find another policy to cover you and the car, which they normally can do, but at much higher cost. For many middle class families trying to pay their bills and save for college, this unexpected expense can be a real problem. Get the picture? Slow down and be careful! Help the people who are trying to help you.

Now we are going to give you some insight into handling a traffic citation. First, you need to take care of it properly. Second, you can merely pay the ticket, but you will have a conviction on your record. If the citation is a moving one, your conviction may result in a driver's license suspension and the possible cancellation of your auto policy (plus the increased cost of another policy). Third, if you got a ticket for no insurance or an expired safety sticker, you may be able to get the ticket dismissed merely by showing up in court, on the date written on the ticket, with a copy of your insurance policy or a paid invoice for a new safety sticker. Fourth, if the ticket is for something else, say speeding, you may be able to get the ticket dismissed by taking "defensive driving," which is a good resolution because it results in the dismissal of the ticket and the lowering of your parents' auto insurance cost (look on the ticket for instructions about taking defensive driving). Fifth, if you were speeding too fast or cited for something that defensive driving can't fix, you can ask the judge to place you on "deferred adjudication," which is probation for a certain time during which you must not violate the law. If you successfully complete the terms of the probation, then the judge will dismiss the ticket. But, if you have had a number of traffic citations within the last year or two, the judge might not give you deferred adjudication, preferring instead to try and teach you a lesson with more severe punishment. Sixth, if you don't fall into one of the above categories, hire a traffic lawyer. They usually are reasonable and can be found in the yellow pages.

If you can't afford a lawyer try this: go to the clerk's office for the court noted on the ticket. Reset your court appearance date. Wait until a week before the new date and repeat the process, resulting in a second reset. Next, show up in court on that second reset date. If the police officer doesn't show up, and many times he or she will not due to confusion or conflicts created by the multiple resetting you did, the court will dismiss the case for lack of evidence. If the police officer does show up, plead not guilty and ask for a jury trial. The prosecutor won't like that because a jury trial in traffic court takes time, and he or she will want to wrap up the docket as fast as possible to get out of court for his or her other business. Therefore, after you ask for a jury trial you can approach the prosecutor and politely try to negotiate a deal, such as probation or a reduced charge, whereby you will plead guilty and the prosecutor can get out of Dodge.

But this resetting approach will not work in cities and counties which have a "pretrial program." A pretrial program is a procedure adopted by some governments to prevent cases from being dismissed by police officers not showing up for trial. In these places the ticket will have a date for you to show up for a pretrial meeting. At that meeting a prosecutor will talk to you and try to work something out. Your best approach here is to show up at the pretrial meeting, dressed like you are going to church (which shows respect and places the prosecutor in a good mood), and be polite. Ask the prosecutor for: first, defensive driving; second, deferred adjudication; or, third, a reduced charge. If the prosecutor agrees, and you committed the offense charged, take the deal. It's the best outcome you can expect. But remember, you must take care of the ticket officially. Otherwise, a warrant will be issued for your arrest. If you are arrested, bail must be posted for your release, and if it's a weekend, your bail may not be set until Monday.

Now, please do not misunderstand our motivation in telling you all of this. We do not recommend that you try and get out of your obligations. Rather, we recommend you be very careful behind the wheel so you do not need to defend a traffic citation. That is the safest, cheapest thing to do (and it avoids your having a migraine over all this stuff).

Consider this: certain states have created traffic point systems, whereby drivers get points for traffic-related crimes, including DWI and DUI. If a driver racks up enough points in a two or three year period, the state charges him or her a fine, up to several thousand dollars per year. Ouch!

Let us turn our attention to curfew laws. Many communities have passed youth curfew laws, providing that persons under a certain age, such as seventeen, cannot be out in public without a parent or guardian in that community after a certain hour, such as 12:00 AM. The reason for these laws is very logical. The cities' officials, and others in the communities, feel that young people are more apt to get in trouble in the very late hours of the night. The problem is that many young people simply don't realize that the police are very serious about enforcing these laws. Most officers are smart about finding kids who think they can break this law. Know what the cops do? They simply wait outside the places kids like to visit at night, like burger joints, bowling alleys, twenty-four hour shopping marts, parks, etc. And guess what happens? You got it. The cops always catch the curfew violators. Some teens don't seem to get it, though. But you never will be charged with a curfew violation, because you read this chapter and have more knowledge than the other kids. The moral here is simple. Obey the law, especially where it's intended to protect you. Just look in the newspaper at all the incidents of foul play that happened the prior day. You know what those are: murders, aggravated assaults, rapes, robberies, and kidnappings. You will see that many of them occurred in the wee hours, that same time you were supposed to be home. Somebody out there wants to separate you from the bad guys. Pay attention.

CHAPTER 8—That tree just fell on my car. What now? (Insurance/Apartment Leases/Credit)

Hopefully, you have insurance to cover that kind of accident. That's why we're presenting this chapter to you. If you understand something about insurance, then maybe you can better protect yourself with it.

One important thing to remember about insurance is that it's not an open checkbook that you casually use when you want some money. It's designed to pay you for a loss that you can't afford to pay yourself. Don't misuse or overuse insurance. Wait for that time when you really need it.

Insurance is normally governed by state law. That is, the laws of each state say how much money insurance companies can charge for policies, what are unfair insurance practices by insurance companies, when and under what circumstances insurance companies must pay disputed claims, what defenses insurance companies can assert to avoid paying disputed claims, and other insurance-related matters. You may have picked up a pattern here: your insurance company isn't your mother. Most insurance companies are "for profit" businesses, meaning they hate paying money to others, like you. But they will do so if the policy calls for it. As a part of understanding insurance, you need to know that you must have the right policies to cover all of the things that can reasonably be expected to happen to you. For example, in that cute little caption in the title of this chapter, where the tree falls on the car, what kind of insurance do you need to pay for that car? If you said "comprehensive," go to the head of the class. You're right. Comprehensive auto insurance pays for loss to your car from things like storms, hail, falling trees, fire, etc. Another type of auto insurance is required for auto loss from accidents with other cars, or telephone poles. This is "collision." And the auto insurance that you are supposed to carry with you or you get a ticket is called "liability," meaning it pays the other guy if you damage his car or hurt him through your fault when driving. There is still another auto insurance that many people carry—"uninsured or underinsured motorist coverage." That pays for your loss if the other guy is at fault but doesn't carry his own liability insurance or only carries a small policy that won't pay enough to cover all of your car and personal injury losses.

There are also insurance policies that cover your parents' home and will pay for the loss of that home from fire or storm (and the loss of the contents from fire, storm, or theft). Usually those policies don't cover mold contamination or loss from flood, and you need separate policies for those problems. That home policy also has liability coverage which will pay for the damages of another person who is hurt at your home, such as the delivery man who slips on the skateboard on your sidewalk and hurts his back.

If you live in an apartment, you can get a renter's policy (at reasonable cost). It will cover the loss of your belongings in the apartment, like furniture, clothing, and TV from fire, theft, storm.

The best advice on getting the insurance you need is to get a good insurance agent and ask for his or her help. A professional insurance agent can explain different types of insurance policies to you and help you collect on disputed claims. But don't be afraid to shop around for an agent you trust (you know—someone who takes your calls, returns your calls, is in the office most of the time, seems to be knowledgeable about insurance matters, seems willing to help you find the right coverage at the best price, etc.). Like lawyers, insurance agents are very different in their knowledge and skill levels. And, different agents have access to different insurance companies, some of which offer more than others. Insurance is expensive and policies vary as to what they will and won't cover and how much they will pay on a loss. It's worth your time to do some comparison shopping.

When you leave home and get a permanent job, you will want to ask about your employer-provided health insurance, which covers medical costs if you are hurt or become sick. It is good to have such insurance because many employer health policies are more easily and economically obtained than individual health policies, meaning policies you get on your own without help from an employer. This is true because employer policies are often called "group health policies," meaning that they cover large groups of people who, together, pay a lot of money to the insurance company for the policy. This, in turn, allows an insurance company to offer a group health policy to all employees, even if those employees couldn't qualify for individual policies, and at lesser cost than individual policies. Another good thing about an employer group health policy is that if you joined such a policy at one employer, then, if you move to another employer, you are guaranteed of being able to join the second employer's group health policy under a federal law called "HIPAA," even if you are sick or pregnant at that time.

During the time you live at home, your parents take care of all the insurance matters. But you need to know about insurance because, even as a teenager, that tree can fall on the car you are paying for, and it is good for you to have the right insurance to fix or replace it.

You might be faced early in your life with renting an apartment, maybe with a roommate. There are a few important points to keep in mind here. First, if you are eighteen or over, you can sign a lease, otherwise, you can't.

Before you sign the lease read it, at least in a general way. The lease is probably fair if it's one that was prepared by an apartment or real estate association. Those leases are used by many apartments. Look at the top of the lease to see if the words "Prepared by the State Apartment Association" or something similar is printed there. If so, you are probably okay in signing the lease. Second, if you and your roommate sign the lease, remember that, most likely, each of you is liable for the entire rent, unless the lease splits the rent obligation between you. So, if your roommate moves out, the apartment will look to you to pay the whole rent until you get another roommate the apartment approves. Third, if you get a new roommate, make him or her sign a document with the apartment manager, naming the new roommate as a renter under the lease. That way he or she will take the lease obligations seriously and, more likely than not, perform them. Fourth, if the apartment is damaged by fire or storm or mechanical failure, you still must pay the rent, unless the apartment is uninhabitable or unsafe, in which event you get a reduction of the rent according to the lease. Fifth, you are entitled to a return of your deposit if you notify the apartment in writing that you will move out when the lease ends (do this within the time stated in the lease, such as one month before the lease ends) and that you want your deposit back. If you do this, then, under the law, the apartment must return your deposit within a short time, such as thirty days, less any amounts needed to repair damages caused by you or for messes you didn't clean up. If the apartment doesn't return your deposit, send a letter demanding return of the deposit. If the apartment still refuses to return the deposit, sue it in small claims court (you will most likely win). Last, please remember that your rent payment obligation affects your credit. If you pay the rent on time, you build good credit; if you don't, you build bad credit.

Since we have finished the apartment section by referring to your credit, let's continue with that subject. You should understand that you build a credit rating based on how you score with a credit agency. You build this score mainly based on one thing—whether you pay your bills on time. If you do that your credit score goes up; if you don't your credit score goes down. So, it's important that you pay your bills when they become due. If you have a problem paying your bills, then do this: talk to the company you are having trouble paying and try to work something out. You can call the customer relations or business office and get in touch with the right person. Don't be shy. This is serious business and you are handling it in a responsible way. When you get in touch with that person, tell him or her your problem and ask that the amount of each payment be reduced to allow you to pay the debt. The company will probably agree because it wants to get paid. If you have something that you can return to reduce your debt, do that right away.

If you recently signed an agreement to buy something, you may be able to cancel it. Consumer protection laws give you the right to cancel consumer contracts up to three business days after you sign it. Do this in writing, faxed or delivered to the selling company. If you do this, the contract is terminated and you don't owe that debt.

You can look at your credit report and correct any inaccurate information, like some company reporting you for not buying something you returned. You get the report from the local credit bureau (look in the phone book).

Last, lock up all your credit cards, except for one emergency card, and don't replace them. They are too easy to use and too costly to pay off. Credit card companies charge very high rates of interest that cost you a bundle if you pay the minimum monthly amount. Remember, your credit score is important. Make the best one you can so that you can buy the things you really need, like a car to get to work.

In this area of paying bills, be aware of three important things: First, it is illegal for a collection agency to engage in unfair debt collection practices, like threatening you with jail for not paying your debts (we don't have debtor's prison in the United States) or calling you late at night or calling your boss or calling you after you asked it not to. If some idiot from a collection agency does any of this stuff, you can sue for violations of the consumer protection laws. You can use small claims court or hire a lawyer. If you win, it's possible to wipe out your debt to that creditor and get your attorney's fees and court costs. Second, if someone sold you something based on a lie, such as an appliance being used when it was supposed to be new, you can sue under the state's deceptive trade practices act. You will need a lawyer here because the formalities of the act can get technical. But, if you win, you can get damages and your attorney's fees and court costs, which may wipe out that debt. Third, and this can be a problem for you, don't write a hot check to pay someone (a hot check is one that you know isn't covered with cash in your account). If you do so, you have violated the criminal law. The other person can file a complaint, and the police will arrest you and make you post a bond to get out of jail. If you make an honest mistake, such as your paycheck bouncing, you probably have a good defense, but don't rely on this. It may or may not work. Be careful with your checking account to insure your checks are covered. Review your bank statement each month for fraudulent checks (ones you didn't sign) and bank fees. Deduct the fees. Immediately write the bank about fraudulent checks. If you do this the bank must credit any such amount to your account.

There is one more thing we need to tell you about credit: you can't merely allow the bank to repossess something you can't pay for. If you do that, then the bank can report to the credit bureau that you didn't pay your debt (which hurts your credit score) and also can sue you for any amount still owing after it sells the thing it repossessed. Therefore, don't just tell the bank, "Come and get the car or refrigerator or TV." Try and work something out with the bank whereby it will agree to satisfy your debt through some program you can do, such as reducing your payment amounts or extending your debt or allowing you to sell the item and pay the proceeds to the bank, etc. This is a much better and more responsible course of action for you. Also, please do not even think of destroying your car to collect insurance or get out of debt. That's a violation of the criminal law and will not help you with you debt problem (the banks and insurance companies have this kind of activity figured out and have investigators to prove it).

We have covered a lot of business law ground, but it's important stuff, everyday reality stuff that you should know and follow to be a good citizen and build a good life. If you need a lawyer for one of these matters and can't afford one, call the local bar association or legal aid association (look in the phone book) for a referral to a lawyer who handles cases for free or on a reduced fee basis. Chances are you will find someone to represent you and get your case handled. The courts love to help people they feel are truly due some justice, particularly those people who appear to be at a disadvantage to a stronger person or a big company. Remember how we started this book, with the discussion about this being a nation of laws. Use the law. It's powerful, and it's there for you.

CHAPTER 9—You mean it's against the law to download music free?
(Copyright law)

Unfortunately for many people who did it, the law makes it illegal to take music from the internet without paying for it. "Why?" you might ask. The reason is because of our copyright laws, which also exist in many other countries. When a person creates an intellectual property, like a song or play or novel or movie script or magazine article, it is covered by federal copyright law. That law says that the creator has the exclusive right to own, control, sell, and make money from his creation. Others cannot take his creation without the creator's permission, and he isn't going to give it to you if you don't pay him something for it. If you violate this copyright law, you can be sued for money damages and prosecuted for a violation of criminal law.

When the internet came into widespread use, some people realized that they could quickly and easily swap information. Some of them began to accumulate many songs in their computers and swap the songs with others, free of cost. This practice spread very fast. Certain kinds of software made the process easier. Do you see a problem here? If you said "yes," then you are paying attention. Well, the recording industry sure saw a problem with this free song swapping practice and responded by filing lots of suits against people involved in it, people who ran companies doing song swapping business, people who provided software to swap songs, people who ran private servers that swapped songs, and people who copied lots of songs for free. Some of these people fought the suits, but they lost. Other people tried to develop screens to hide their identities on the internet, but technology soon broke through those screens, allowing the recording industry to find out who those people were and sue them.

The moral here is simple: you don't get something worth having for free. Pay for your songs and don't get caught up in this mess.

There's another concept you need to know in this area of intellectual property law and that's what is called "plagiarism." When you are doing a paper for school and conducting research for that paper, you are going to run across all kinds of information, even some papers on the same subject. It is against the law to take someone else's work and pass it off as your work. The correct way to handle placing someone else's work in your paper: 1. you can get written permission to quote someone's work, or 2. you can use a small part of it for educational purposes and give credit to that other person in your paper, such as in a footnote (this is called "fair use").

However, you can see that if you get a paper by another person and put your name on it as the author, then you have committed plagiarism. Additionally, you may not know this, but many colleges and high schools have purchased internet searching software to check suspicious papers against everything on the web to locate copied works by other authors. This software is pretty accurate and catches things like similar wording, style, content, ideas. It can locate papers on subjects like yours. If you copied another person's work or used it too closely, you could get an F on a term paper, fail the class, and get in trouble with the school for copying another person's work. That is really stupid when it's so easy to put ideas in your own words and deliver a unique paper. After all, you have a mind of your own, don't you? If you have an idea that turns out to be like that in another paper, think of a new twist or argument. Then expand on your new idea. Result: you learn something, feel good about yourself, and develop expertise in a special area. Doesn't that sound good?

CHAPTER 10—You want me to do what? (Employment law)

You need to know something about our labor laws, mainly because many teens get jobs. It's unfortunate to say, but some employers may treat young people unfairly, assigning them to improper jobs and underpaying them for their work. Pay attention and learn your rights in this area.

All of the states have labor laws, and the federal government does, too. These laws directly affect teen workers, mainly because they are intended to protect workers from improper or unfair labor practices. Here are some of the more important labor law rules you should know:

1. Minimum Wages—These laws set certain minimum
   wages that employers, as a general rule, must pay.
   Presently, the federal minimum wages are $7.25 per
   hour as the basic national minimum wage; $2.13 per
   hour for tipped employees; and $4.25 for people
   under twenty years old, but only during the first ninety
   days of employment (this is called the "opportunity
   wage"). Employers may pay a sub-minimum wage, if
   they obtain written permission from the U. S.
   Department of Labor, to disabled people with reduced
   earning ability, apprentices, messengers, learners, full
   time students working as retail or service workers,
   agricultural workers, college employees, and
   elementary or secondary school employees. But
   remember, the employer can't just say that it has the
   right to pay this sub-minimum wage. It must have
   written permission to do so. You may ask to see that
   permission. The laws of certain states can affect the
   minimum wage, and, generally, those laws must be
   followed by employers if they produce a more
   favorable result for the employee. For example,
   Minnesota, Washington, Montana, Nevada, Oregon,
   Alaska, and California do not allow any tipped
   employee to be paid below the minimum wage;
   California's is $8.00; Colorado sets a $7.28 minimum;
   Connecticut's minimum wage is $8.00; DC's minimum
   wage is $8.25; Illinois has an $8.00 minimum; Maine's
   is $7.50; Massachusetts has an $8.00 wage floor;
   Michigan's minimum is $7.40; New Mexico uses

$7.50; Ohio sets a minimum of $7.30; Oregon requires at least $8.40; Rhode Island sets $7.40 as the minimum; Vermont requires at least $8.06; Washington state provides an $8.55 minimum. In the other states, use the federal minimum wage, above noted. Some large cities may provide their own minimum wages. To see if your city has a minimum wage, call the city attorney's office. There are very detailed and complex other rules affecting the minimum wage, such as the employer being able to count the value of meals or uniforms it provides toward its employee minimum-required compensation. It would be unworkable to cover those rules here (you wouldn't read all that stuff). Just remember that, as a general rule, you should be paid the minimum amount for your state and type of job. If you feel you aren't being paid the proper wage, contact the local office of the U. S. Department of Labor or your state agency on workers' rights for help (see Appendix Two for information on such agencies).

2. Overtime pay—Just like in the minimum wage area, federal and state law apply here, too. The law that does best for the employee will be followed, and these states have overtime laws that may add to federal law rights or be more favorable to employees than federal law: AK, CA, CO, CT, FL, HI, IL, KY, ME, MA, MI, MN, MT, ND, NV, OR, and VT. Check with your state workers' rights agency, listed in Appendix Two, about

your state's overtime rules. Under federal law, overtime is any time actually worked over forty hours per week. If the employee works more than forty hours per week, he or she is to be paid time and a half for each overtime hour worked that week. Exceptions to this federal law include salaried employees who meet a certain legal test (which is that the employee's main job must involve the exercise of discretion and independent judgment concerning important matters—basically, you must have a management or professional job), and railroad, theater, domestic, taxi driver, agricultural, auto/truck dealer, TV/radio announcer, and airline employees. In other words, those employees aren't required to be paid enhanced wages by the employer for their overtime, unless, of course, state law requires that they be paid extra for it. If in doubt, check with the Department of Labor or your state workers' rights agency (see Appendix Two for their telephone numbers).

3. Deductions from pay—Federal and state laws regulate this area, and they vary somewhat. The basic rule you need to know here is simply this: your employer, as a general rule, can't deduct amounts from your pay, other than normal payroll taxes and amounts you authorize in writing to be deducted, like health insurance premiums. Some employers try to deduct amounts they claim someone stole or the value of a broken or missing tool. Normally, they can't legally

make such deductions without your written permission. If your employer does this, complain to your state agency for workers' rights (see Appendix Two for information on those agencies). Do not give such permission to your employer if you feel that you aren't responsible for the loss it wants to collect from you. The rules relating to commissions and expense account reimbursements are different and generally turn on the agreement between the employer and the employee. These matters usually don't come up in teen employment situations.

4. Timing of pay—State law regulates this area under what are commonly called "payday laws." Basically, your employer can't hold your pay for a long time but, in many states, must pay at least twice a month. Additionally, when you leave, the employer must pay you no later than the next scheduled payday. While state laws may vary these rules somewhat, they are generally true. If the employer waits much beyond these times to pay you, call the local office of your state workers' rights agency, and they can help you get paid (see Appendix Two for your state agency).

5. Hazardous duty—Unfortunately, some employers push young employees to do most of the less appealing jobs, claiming the more senior employees get more favorable jobs. This is okay for some jobs, like sweeping the floor, washing dishes, cleaning leaves from a walkway, painting a fence, etc. But it is

not okay if the employee is asked to perform a hazardous job and he or she is under a certain age. For example, under federal law, a person under eighteen may not work in jobs involving: radiation, excavation, explosives, the operation of certain power equipment, logging/saw mills, mining, meat processing, big motor rigs, roofing, and demolition. Additionally, under the federal Occupational Safety and Health Administration laws, even if you are eighteen, the employer must protect you from hazardous conditions, such as: high work places (fall protection), trenches in the ground (shoring of the hole), metal grinding (eye protection), dusty or foul air (breathing protection), open gears or pinch points (machinery guards covering dangerous parts), and loud noises (hearing protection). Also, there are state laws that impose their own hazardous job limitations, and you should contact your state workers' rights agency about these laws (see Appendix Two for your state's agency). If you are asked to work in unsafe conditions, you may also call the U. S. Department of Labor or the Occupational Safety and Health Administration (see Appendix Two for information on these agencies). Their local offices are listed in your phone book, and they take safety matters very seriously.

6. Termination and discrimination—You need to know that, generally, it is illegal, even in the so called

"employment at will" states, for an employer to terminate or refuse to hire you based on any of the following: age (unless you are younger than 14, working in a non-agricultural job and lied about your age), gender, religion, nationality, ethnicity, disability, or filing a worker's compensation claim for being hurt on the job. Some of these laws, however, do not apply to employers with fewer than fifteen employees, and there are other limitations to these laws as well. If you feel that you have been improperly terminated or refused employment, call the U. S. Department of Labor or the U. S. Equal Employment Opportunity Commission or your state workers' rights agency (see Appendix Two for information on these agencies). They have expert people who will tell you whether you have been illegally fired or refused employment, and they will help you if the employer violated the law.

7. Hurt on the job—The states have laws called "workers' compensation" statutes, and they provide that an injured worker will be taken care of by the employer, no matter whether or not anyone was at fault in causing the accident that hurt the employee. Some big employers pay the employee's medical bills themselves and some other employers have insurance. The injured employee usually gets payments for doctor's bills, rehabilitation costs, and lost wages, up to a certain limit. If you are hurt, tell your boss right away in order to participate in this

program. There are two more things you need to know here: one—some employers don't have a workers' compensation program even though they should (it's not a good idea to work for someone like that); and two—if you get high on alcohol or drugs and cause the accident that hurts you on the job, the workers' compensation program won't cover your losses and costs (another good reason to avoid alcohol and illegal drugs).

8. Sickness—If you get sick and your employer has at least fifteen employees, you have the right to take off up to twelve weeks from work without pay to get well. You then may come back to work to your old job or a similar one. These rights fall under the Family and Medical Leave Act designed to protect employees' jobs when they have a medical reason for leaving work (or the birth or adoption of a child). If a situation such as this arises, tell your employer you need to take up to twelve weeks off. You may need to provide a doctor's report to support your leave. But your job will be protected under the law.

This is only a small amount of the law relating to labor matters. For example, there are federal and state laws covering the maximum number of hours that a teen may work, depending on his/her age and specific job. Other laws, state and federal, cover time off and rest time (coffee breaks). The basic rule here is that, generally, employees are entitled to some time off and to breaks during the day. You may contact the Department of Labor or your state workers' rights agency for information about these areas of the law.

There are lawyers who spend a career practicing in the labor law specialty, and it is very complex and ever changing. However, you don't necessarily need an employment lawyer to resolve your claim. State and federal government offices can help you for free. If you think that you have been wronged in this area you may call the U. S. Department of Labor, the U. S. Equal Employment Opportunity Commission or your state agency on workers' rights. If you still need a lawyer call your local bar association (normally listed in the phone book such as "Houston Bar Association") for a "pro bono" lawyer (that's a lawyer who takes a certain number of cases for free as a benefit for the community's less affluent citizens). There are also legal aid organizations in many cities and counties. These provide lawyers for free or on a reduced fee basis. Look in your phone book for the nearest legal aid organization. Any of these offices is a good place to start and may correct the situation or explain why your legal rights were not violated, if that is the case.

There are legal remedies if you are not treated fairly at work. But, our advice is simply this: make yourself as valuable an employee as possible; get all of the education and training you can; tell the truth, work hard, and follow the law. If you do these things, you will find that, more often than not, your value as an employee will prevent employment problems from arising (the employer will really need you).

CHAPTER 11—Who's going to pay for my injuries? (Others causing injuries and damages to you)

We've talked a lot about your being careful and not hurting the other person. But what happens when another person hurts you? How do you get paid, and what can you get paid for? You must remember that just because you are a minor (under eighteen) you still have rights to be compensated when another person wrongs you and causes damages.

We have spoken of an employee's legal rights, and you should have some basic understanding of that matter. If not, read the prior chapter again.

In the area of business, contracts are the basic way people operate. But you are a minor, and minors can't legally enter into a contract. So, if you want to buy something that requires a contract or make some business deal, have your parents act for you. That way you will have a legal contract and can enforce it through your parents. The way you enforce a contract is quite simple. You merely file a lawsuit and say that you had a contract, the other guy didn't follow it, you did everything you were supposed to do, and the other guy's breach of contract cost you money. Then you tell the judge how much you lost and let him do the rest. If your evidence is the more credible (the other person, the "defendant," will probably have some excuse for not performing the contract) you win and the judge will sign a "judgment" ordering the other guy to pay you. You can then take that judgment and give it to a lawyer for collection. The judgment is usually good for ten years. You will need to use a lawyer to collect the judgment because collection laws are technical. You can wait until you are eighteen to hire a lawyer for this purpose. The judgment probably will have been obtained by your parents since they were on the contract, but they can assign it to you when you turn eighteen (it's a valuable property, the money from which you can collect in the future).

In the personal injury area, many times the other fellow has insurance to pay the judgment. If you are hurt, such as in a car wreck, and the insurance company pays off, then you get your money right away. If the insurance company won't pay before a lawsuit, then, if you are younger than eighteen, your parent will sue for you as "next friend." Many personal injury lawyers will take these cases on "contingency," meaning you don't have to pay the lawyer's fee up front but the lawyer will get his money out of the recovery from the insurance company, if any. You can find a lawyer in the phone book or from the referral service of your local bar association. Basically, you can recover money for physical pain and suffering, mental trauma, impairment, disfigurement, lost wages and diminished earning capacity, loss of use of property (or the reasonable cost of renting replacement property while yours is being fixed), and property damage and destruction.

If you win the case, then the court will have a separate attorney approve the final outcome of the case for you; this other attorney is called an "attorney ad litem." Because you are a minor, your money will usually be placed in a trust until you are eighteen. This trust can be handled by the clerk of the court or by a bank or an insurance company or a relative. Let us mention one word of caution here. Most parents are loving, caring people but are strapped for cash. It is not a good idea to let your parents care for your big chunk of money that you got from the insurance company. Sometimes this money disappears as the parents use it to raise the family. Therefore, you should insist to the attorney ad litem or the judge that the money be controlled by someone other than your parents, preferably a private institution, such as a bank or insurance company. These institutions are controlled by laws requiring their honesty and competence in handling your money. (Don't say that you don't trust your parents. Merely say that banks and insurance companies handle money as a part of their business and you prefer to let the experts handle yours, for your future.) You will find that the money will be there for you when you turn eighteen and that the private institution is faster and easier to deal with than government people, like clerks of courts.

You should know something about how our courts are structured. There are federal courts and state courts. The federal ones handle larger civil cases, cases involving federal questions, and federal criminal cases. You probably would not bring your civil case in a federal court. State courts are usually divided into two major areas, civil law and criminal law. Your civil case will, most likely, be filed in a state civil court. Those courts are divided into different levels, with the lowest level being the small claims courts, the next level being the trial courts for moderate amounts (county courts), and the top trial courts being for really large amounts (district courts). The small claims courts can be useful for many disputes. The law says that the small claims court is supposed to do justice, without a lot of legal formality or the need for an attorney. You, or your parent if you are under eighteen, can sue without a lawyer in a small claims court if the amount you are seeking is no more than a certain amount, such as $10,000. The way you do this is simple. Go to the clerk of the small claims court near you (look in the front of your phone book for that information). Then go see that clerk and tell him or her that you want to file a civil suit. The clerk will tell you how much you can sue for in that court. If your claim is not more than that amount, then you fill out a form, a "complaint," listing your name and address and that same information for the guy you are suing, the "defendant," pay a small fee to file the case with the clerk and have the constable or sheriff serve your complaint on the defendant, and wait. In a few weeks you will get word from the clerk that the case is set for trial on a certain date, at a particular time. Be in the court then, with all papers and pictures proving your case. Take your parent if you're under eighteen. When your name is called, go stand before the judge (smile politely and refer to the judge as "Your Honor;" they like that). Tell the judge what happened. Don't be afraid; formal rules of evidence and procedure don't apply. Just put your story in your own words. Chances of your winning are pretty good if you have a legitimate claim. If you win, the judge will sign a judgment ordering the defendant to pay you. After that, if the defendant doesn't voluntarily pay, you can pay a small fee to the clerk and get a "Writ of Execution" that the constable will take to the defendant to try and collect your judgment. If that doesn't work (the defendant might say he's broke), give the judgment to an attorney for collection. It's also possible that after you sue the defendant, he will pay you before the trial just to end the case and not go before the judge.

A short word is appropriate about investing. We are not giving you investment advice, which can be rendered only by licensed investment advisors. Rather, we intend only to give you a general understanding of the subject. Investing can be complicated and risky. Some people have lost a lot of money doing it, while others have made money. When it comes to your money, remember that you don't need to take any crazy risks with it. You are young, and a little money invested over time usually results in a pot of gold later. So what do you look for as investments and what do you avoid? Some people like to invest in "certificates of deposit" or "CDs" as they are commonly called. These are like savings accounts and grow from the interest that the principal earns. The upside is that they do not go down in value, like stocks can. Also, they are insured up to a certain amount, meaning if the bank fails, you get that amount from the federal government for your CD in that bank. The downside is that CDs are conservative investments, many times earning less than more aggressive investments. "Stocks" represent ownership in a company, while "bonds" represent a debt of a company or other entity. "Blue chip" stocks can be a good bet. They are the stocks of the big, historically strong companies. Some are in energy; others are in computer software or hardware; still others are in electronics or consumer goods. "Mutual funds" can be good investments. Those are companies that own the stocks of many other companies. They spread their risk among many businesses and buy and sell different stocks from time to time. Some mutual funds specialize in certain industries, such as high tech companies. Therefore, if a particular industry is strong, you may want to buy a mutual fund that invests in that industry. T Bills or Treasury Bills are thought to be safe because they are backed by the federal government. T Bills work this way: you buy one for a certain amount of money and, after several years, you cash it in at any bank for a higher amount. "Government bonds" can be good, and some of them are tax free, meaning you don't pay income tax on the gain you get from the bond when it comes due ("matures"). Be careful about: church bonds (churches may or may not have the money to pay the bond when it comes due), so called "penny stocks" (these are companies with very low stock prices because their financial performances are questionable), companies in struggling industries that might be overcrowded with competitors, companies with legal problems, and small family owned companies that are not publicly traded (this kind of company can escape the control of officials who protect the investing public). We tell you this information because if you invest unwisely, your money could be lost. Talk to the bank about your investing options and make sure they are putting your money in sound investments. Additionally, when you turn eighteen, you may still want to keep investing your nest egg, and it will be good if you know a little about the subject. Warning: ask the bank about management fees and how to reduce them, like buying mutual funds with lower fees.

Before you start counting the money, remember the "statute of limitations." These are laws placing a time limit on how long you have to file suit after the date of the wrong. They vary by state. If you go over these limits your case may be dismissed by the court on motion by the defendant. Here are the time limits for various claims in Texas: contract claims, four years; fraud claims, four years; tort claims, two years; defamation claims, one year. Generally, if you're under eighteen, the time starts when you reach eighteen.

Automobiles always seem to present problems, and we will cover some of the more common problems here. If you buy a new car, it is a good idea to take an adult with you to review the sales contract before you sign it, assuming you are at least eighteen. While many car dealers are honest, some aren't and have been known to change terms in the sales contract, like the final price, after the parties agreed to the terms of the deal. Extended warranties can be a good investment, but make the dealer give you something in writing explaining in detail what that warranty covers. Some of them aren't good buys because they cover things that normally don't go out, like the transmission or engine block or heads. Before you buy that extended warranty, ask the dealer whether it covers things likely to break during the extended time period. Used cars can be a good buy, but you need to check them out closely. The best bet is to buy the used car from a business that sells used cars with a certificate of inspection, saying the car was checked and found to be sound, and with a warranty. Avoid buying from people you don't know, unless you get the used car checked by a mechanic and he says it is in good running order. But understand that a car warranty is valuable because it gives you specific rights to sue if the warranty isn't honored (and you can also get attorney's fees and court costs when you sue for breach of warranty and win the case). Therefore, get that warranty whenever possible. When you pay your car off, the bank should sign the original title, which it holds, saying the loan was paid. If you don't get that title, call the bank and complain. Hopefully, you will get the original title in the mail in a few days. Look to make sure the bank signed the title releasing its lien. If so, your title is then clear and evidences your ownership of the car. Put the title in a safe place (you will need it when you sell the car). If the title is lost, you can file an affidavit with your state department of motor vehicles, and they will issue you a replacement title. A form and a fee are required for this service (get the form from the local government office that handles car titles; many times it is the county tax office).

Lemon laws are designed for the return of new, defective cars. But they are hyped and have little practical benefit for the normal consumer. The reason for this problem is that the auto dealers have influenced the state legislators to water down these laws to make them toothless. For example, if the car you own is a lemon, it's logical to assume that the car dealer should be required to return your money under the Lemon law. But there is a catch: the dealer gets a credit for the time you drove the car and the miles you put on it and any damage you did to it. Therefore, he really owes you little or nothing under the refund formula in the Lemon law. To get a fairer result, it is better to use the Deceptive Trade Practices Act ("DTPA"). That is the law that lets you sue if someone lies or tricks you in a commercial sale. Thus, if the dealer told you that the car was great, reliable, durable, long lasting, advanced in every way, designed and made better than others, and it turns out the car is really a heap, you can sue the dealer for lying. You get your damages, attorney's fees and court costs if you win. If the dealer intentionally lied, you may be able to recover additional damages (which are a multiple of your actual damages, like 3 X the amount of money the dealer's lies cost you), sometimes referred to as "treble damages." You will need a lawyer for this type of suit. But a letter from him or her (and you must send a letter at least thirty days before you sue under the DTPA) can do wonders to get you some serious attention from the dealer who ignored you in the past.

We hope you now understand something about your legal rights when another person does you wrong. The laws are designed to level things out and compensate people for their losses. The key is knowing what to do, how to do it, how you can get some help, and how long you have to take the right legal action.

CHAPTER 12—You mean there are more laws to talk about? (Some sneaky criminal laws)

There are other important rules to cover, laws that can affect your life dramatically, and no overview of the law would be complete without mentioning them. Here they are:

A. Did you know that in some states a minor caught with a gun can be jailed without a trial, until a hearing is held to determine whether or not he or she is a danger to society? This law is the result of increased public alarm over the escalating number of gun-related deaths involving minors. Also in the gun law area, it is against federal law to possess certain high kill weapons without a special license, like machine guns, automatic rifles, missile launchers, hand grenades, and sawed-off shotguns. Federal agents have a habit of tracing the sales of such items and filing criminal weapons charges against violators.

B. Jokes concerning guns, bombs, killings, etc. are not considered funny by the police. In fact, if you say such things at airports, you will surely be detained by the airport police and questioned until they are sure you are not a security threat (and you'll probably miss your plane).

C. If you should get mad and phone a bomb threat to a school or government office, you have just committed a terrorist crime that can be a felony if you hurt someone or interfered with a government-related activity. In this same vein, it is a crime to threaten a public official with violence. Comments about violent acts toward such people can land you in jail. If you should try to carry out such a threat, then you are in far worse trouble. It can be a felony to assault a police officer. So, don't scuffle with a police officer who stops you, even if you feel he or she wasn't justified in doing so. Additionally, it is a specific crime to point a laser beam at a police officer (lasers can damage the eye), and such behavior also is probably an assault against the officer and any civilian citizen, for which you can be charged with a criminal offense.

D. Have you ever heard the saying, "You might beat the rap but you won't beat the ride?" That simply means you shouldn't resist an arrest by a police officer, because, to do so is a separate criminal offense, even if the underlying charge is dismissed. If an officer stops you, don't get cute; don't fight the officer; don't try to get away; and don't make stupid jokes that could be construed as threats. Be polite and cooperative and do what the officer directs (this doesn't mean you should admit to a crime—you still have the right not to incriminate yourself; don't admit anything to the officer). This way you won't create any more trouble that can be used against you. After you are released, you and your attorney can plan a defense against the, hopefully, single charge resulting from the stop.

E. You need to understand the basics of "search and seizure" law. The Fourth Amendment to the United States Constitution prohibits government police and agents from engaging in unreasonable searches and seizures in places where we expect privacy, like our houses, apartments, businesses, cars, purses, pockets, etc. These rules do not apply to private security guards (so, don't think you can get away with criminal activity around private security guards; they may get evidence against you that a police officer could not legally get). As a general rule, a police officer needs either a court issued warrant or "probable cause" to stop, arrest, or search you or to seize evidence from private places (we'll give you the exceptions to this rule later). If the police violate this rule, the prosecutor cannot use any evidence the police found when they violated the rule. This means the officer must have some reasonable indication that a crime was committed or is being committed, or that there is evidence of criminal activity in a certain place to get a warrant or to stop/arrest/search you without a warrant. It doesn't make any difference, however, that the crime might be a small one, like failing to wear your seat belt. Even for very small violations of the law an officer can stop and arrest you. During the stop, the officer can search you and the area immediately around you (the area you can reach) and use any evidence he/she finds as the basis of the crime for which you were stopped or another crime (example: if you were stopped for speeding and the officer finds heroine in your pocket you can be charged with speeding and possession of an illegal drug). If the officer has additional probable cause to believe another crime was or is being committed he/she can conduct a wider search than the area immediately around you. Let's illustrate this situation with a car: the officer stops you for speeding; he/she sees fresh blood on the back seat (it's legal for the officer to peer into the windows of the car and to shine a flashlight into the car); the officer can search the entire car; and the prosecutor can use any evidence the officer finds in the car, such as a body in the trunk.

You probably picked up on the fact that a police officer doesn't need a search warrant to search your car, assuming he/she had probable cause to stop you in the first place or some reasonable suspicion something illegal might be going on. If the officer were to leave to get the warrant, the car would be gone when he or she got back; that's why the officer doesn't need to get a search warrant for a car. However, as we showed you, that search is limited to the area you can reach in the car (front seat, front floorboards, glove box, etc.), unless you give the officer reason to believe something illegal is going on somewhere else in the car. What can give the officer that belief? These things can: the sight of a gun, illegal drugs, a large amount of cash, or the smell of marijuana or alcohol. Therefore, in the event a police officer stops you for some traffic violation and he/she has probable cause of some other crime in the car, a warrantless search of you and the entire car may be legally proper, not just those places in the car that you can reach. In that situation, any evidence found anywhere in that car can be used against you. And remember, an officer can legally stop you for playing your radio too loud, which is a violation of noise ordinances found in towns and cities across the country. It is also illegal in some states to use a cell phone when you are driving, which, of course, gives the officer the right to stop you and search the area around you in the car.

F. We spoke of certain exceptions to the need for the police to have probable cause to stop, search, or arrest a person. In the car situation here are some of those exceptions: 1. you fit a criminal profile, like a young male driving late at night in a high crime area (race cannot be an element of a profile; if it is, this exception does not apply); 2. traffic stops to check for illegal immigrants; 3. an indication that something suspicious is going on, like you speed up at the sight of a police car or you act nervously when a police cruiser pulls up alongside of you at a stop light or you throw something out of the car when you see a policeman in a car.

G. Search warrants are normally required of homes and businesses. However, if a police officer sees a crime being committed, he or she can pursue the suspect into a home or business without any warrant. This is called the "hot pursuit" doctrine. The same holds true if an officer sees a criminal act being committed in a home or business, such as through a window, which is called the "plain view" doctrine. The hot pursuit and plain view doctrines are additional exceptions to the need for police to have a warrant for a stop, search, or arrest.

H. You should also be aware that if an officer is legally in a home or business (such as with an arrest warrant or under the plain view doctrine) the officer has the legal right to search the immediate area around the person he/she is investigating or arresting. This is called a "protective sweep" and is intended to protect the officer from items and people in hiding which might be a danger to him/her or prevent the destruction of evidence. Any evidence found in this protective sweep, even though the officer had no search warrant, can be used in court against you. Just as in the car situation, if the officer sees something to give him or her reason to believe something illegal is happening elsewhere in the house, the officer can expand the search and use any evidence he or she finds.

I. It is important that you know illegally gotten evidence, such as when a warrant was necessary but not obtained or during an illegal stop or from an excessive search, cannot be used against you, even if that evidence is very powerful (like the illegal drug you are charged with possessing). This is called the "exclusionary rule" and has been used in countless cases to exclude damaging evidence and set the defendant free.

J. If you are at the border of our country, and being at the border means at the real border or at an airport or at a seaport, then the police don't need probable cause to search you and your luggage but can search if they have what is called "reasonable suspicion." The law gives police greater rights to enforce the law at the country's borders, largely because those are vulnerable points where people can smuggle drugs or weapons or prohibited items in or out of the country. So, don't bring illegal things to any such places. Chances are you will look guilty and the police will get suspicious and search you. This is also true if someone asks you to carry his package onto an airplane. If that package contains something illegal, like drugs, then you are responsible, even if you didn't know the contents. There is also a nasty problem with carrying a lot of cash when you travel: U. S. customs agents think a person carrying a big wad of money is probably related to illegal drug sales = you get stopped and searched and questioned; also, some foreign countries make it illegal to bring a large amount of foreign currency into their countries, and they will confiscate the cash and arrest you. Tell your friend you can't bring that bag of money to his uncle in Mexico, but that he needs to make other arrangements. That's just being smart (because you read this book).

K. Here's another good rule: don't use your computer to make threats or harass someone or say illegal things or swap copyrighted material or engage in any pornographic activities (it's against the law to possess child pornography). The police can trace such activities and find you, even if you think you have shielded your identity, and charge you with a crime. Don't put illegal material on your or your parents' computer, even if you later delete it. There are recovery programs investigators use to recall material from memory, even deleted or changed information.

L. Also, drag racing is a crime, not merely a traffic violation. If your race hurts or kills someone or results in a wreck, then the charge is more serious, probably a felony. Even merely being a spectator of a drag race can get you charged with a crime. Avoid this activity. You are not a trained race driver, and your car, no matter how hot, is not designed to be a race car.

M. Crimes of moral turpitude are especially bad news because they reflect on a person's basic honesty, which can mean that the person can't get a job that requires honesty, such as a job with a bank or a police force or with the government or with a security firm. In fact, you should be aware that a lawyer can lose his or her license to practice law for the conviction of a crime of moral turpitude. And what are such crimes? They include theft, forgery, shoplifting, theft of services (like when you steal cable service from your neighbor's cable box and the cable company detects the theft with equipment designed for that purpose), lying to a police officer, or lying in court (called "perjury"). Avoid these crimes at all cost. They can ruin your future career plans.

N. Be aware that convictions under state theft statutes are especially dangerous. The reason is because many such laws say that theft convictions can be added together and when you get to a certain number of convictions, say three, you can be charged with a felony even if the individual values of the things you stole are small (a $10 CD plus a $5 lipstick plus a $2 candy bar = a felony). Don't shoplift! Many stores will prosecute, even for small thefts, because they are tired of getting ripped off.

O. It is also very dangerous to bring a weapon (gun, knife, brass knuckles) onto government property, especially if you are trespassing (like being on school property after hours or in a public park after it is closed or in a part of a government building that is off limits to the general public). Some states provide that you can be charged with a felony for doing this.

P. Have you ever had the urge to scribble your protests on a wall or road or public sign, such as, "The government sucks?" Well, forget it. This harmless-sounding activity, commonly known as "writing or drawing graffiti," can get you in big trouble. You probably know that the police can charge you with criminal mischief, which may not scare you. But did you know that you could also be charged with a felony, maybe even manslaughter? If you write graffiti on a public traffic sign, like a speed limit placard, you could be charged with a felony. You can easily see why, can't you? And, if you and your friends should be foolish enough to paint over a stop sign or one of those traffic mirrors in a parking garage, well, you get the picture. So think before you write on something that is supposed to protect people. If you have an urge to draw, paint or scribble something, take an art class.

Q. Similarly, vandalism is no harmless prank. It's a criminal act. People have received fines and prison time for keying cars, smashing windows and spray painting walls.

Additionally, the property owner can sue you and your parents for his damages, and insurance companies can also sue to recover paid claims.

R. A word about hazing is in order: DON'T! Many states have laws making it illegal, even a felony, to haze someone. Some misinformed people think it's cool or a mark of brotherhood/sisterhood to make someone drink alcohol until he/she passes out or do some dangerous thing (cross that highway on foot to show you are brave). Here's the straight and skinny on that stuff: it's stupid, doesn't prove anything good, and is illegal. In a real case, the pledge class leader of a college fraternity got jail time for promoting alcohol consumption that led to the death of a pledge. And, in a high school case, members of a club were prosecuted for hazing a new member.

S. Military law is a body of rules that applies only to military personnel. Before you enlist, other federal laws may apply to you. What you should know is this: 1. you are not required to enlist in the military; we have a voluntary military; 2. if you are a guy, you need to register with the Selective Service when you turn eighteen, which you can do online or at a post office; 3. the military might be good for a guy or girl because it allows you to mature, gives you life skills, provides you a career path (if you choose to stay in the military), gives you a great retirement package, and will pay for your college education; 4. there is no requirement that you go see a military recruiter or keep an appointment with one; so, do not let a recruiter intimidate you into believing you need to come see him or sign up (there is no law requiring such things); 5. if you do enlist, take your service seriously and finish your term; being AWOL can lead to jail time; also, receiving a dishonorable discharge can hurt your later opportunities in civilian life.

T. Interstate commerce is a concept you should understand because in involves the application of federal law. The United States Constitution contains the "Commerce Clause" which applies federal law to those activities involving interstate commerce, basically people or things moving between two or more states. The relevant part for you is this: if you should engage in wrongdoing that crosses a state line, you have just brought U. S. federal law into play. When you do this, the federal officials get involved, and they bring the weight of federal resources to bear on the matter, like the FBI. If, for example, you should wiretap a conversation between two people, U. S. wiretap criminal laws apply (phone lines run across state borders); if you illegally take a child from one state to another, federal kidnapping law applies; if you have a support obligation and move to another state, federal criminal nonsupport charges can be filed; hack into a computer, and U. S. anti-hacking statutes come into play (remember the phone lines). The important aspect of all this is to know that once you cross a state's border, and you are doing anything illegal, you have triggered federal law and opened the door for federal authorities to take action. The feds tend to take these matters seriously; their laws can be harsh; their judges have great power; and they will not treat you like your momma does.

U. Today's fancy copiers have led some kids to counterfeit currency. It seems that the copiers are so good, especially when computer enhanced, they can reproduce most of the markings and colors on genuine bills. This should not really take much explanation. DO NOT DO THIS, NO MATTER HOW APPEALING IT SEEMS! The Secret Service, acting under authority from the Department of Treasury, takes a very dim view of this practice. They will find you and prosecute. If that doesn't scare you, reread paragraph T. above, and keep reading it until you get scared and forget about trying to make a few illegal bucks that will be eaten up by the thousands of dollars you will pay a lawyer to keep you out of federal prison.

V. Picture this: you are a star athlete; people are falling all over you, buying you stuff and offering you money and cars to attend various universities; a professional sports agent even approached you with an offer of representation; maybe you will get a fat shoe deal, when you are a professional star, that is. Man, could life be any sweeter? Now, here is the reality: Most states have laws regulating amateur athletes in certain sports, like football and basketball. The reason for these laws is to protect young athletes from being exploited (used) by profit-seekers. The basic thing to remember is it's illegal to offer or accept anything of value for an amateur's athletic performance, such as a car to attend a particular university. Anyone who does this can be prosecuted, and you could also be prosecuted and lose your amateur athletic status, meaning you might not be allowed to play college ball or get a scholarship. The hard truth is that of all the thousands of gifted athletes in high school, only a very few make it in professional athletics. You might say, "So what's the legal part of that?" Here it is: If you stay in school, complete your studies, get a good job, and play the odds in your favor, you are much more likely to follow the law than the guy who got hyped to ignore school because of the possibility of becoming a professional athlete but didn't make it. That guy has few options, and desperate people do bad things. But you are not desperate because you stayed in school, studied, got your degree, became a lawyer, got a good job, and follow the rules, including the times you nudge the speed limit just a bit, to feel the power of your new sports car (but you know not to get that speeding ticket, because you read this book).

W. You have heard it said that if you are being investigated with a crime you should, "Take the Fifth." That advice is accurate and is based on our legal guarantee against self-incrimination under the Fifth Amendment to the United States Constitution. That guarantee should be used unless you strike a good deal with the prosecutor or a judge gives you immunity and orders you to spill the beans. However, there is a related matter that you should consider: whenever you are talking to a police officer or to a government investigator, and you are not the target of the investigation, and you are not guilty of anything related to the investigation, it is essential that you be cooperative and truthful with the investigator. The reason for this recommendation is that it is a separate crime for you to lie to an official investigator, state or federal, even if the underlying charge has nothing to do with you. This law is related to the one that makes it a crime to make a false report or 911 call. You can see that if people lie to the police, they would have a very difficult time doing their jobs. You may have even heard of someone who got jail time, not for the underlying charge, but, rather, for lying to the investigating agent. If you are unsure about whether or not your comments will be used against you, do not lie to the officer. Assert your Fifth Amendment rights and seek the advice of a lawyer.

X. It is important to discuss terrorism and hate crimes. Terrorism involves creating terror in others to further some illegal purpose. It can involve threats of bombs, gas, poison, guns, or death to: disrupt government functions (including schools), influence legitimate activities, or spread panic among a group of people. Hate crimes occur when a person uses some socially intolerable means (burning crosses, hateful signs, hangman's noose, threatening letter) to further an illegal, hateful intent to harm others. An ordinary criminal charge can be increased to a more serious charge if a hate crime is also involved (you beat up someone because of his race or national origin). Terrorism and hate crimes are viewed as especially bad because they have no rational basis and can cause devastating personal harm to others. In fact, these crimes can be charged as felonies. Avoid participating in such conduct, even if you are kidding. You may have heard of the Patriot Act, which was enacted after the terrible events of September 11, 2001. That law tries to strengthen our nation against terrorist criminals. Here's the part you need to remember: stay away from conduct that could bring that law against you: phone threats to your school or an airline; threatening someone with a bomb. If you want to express your strong opinion about some social issue, do it legally: run for political office when you become an adult or support a political candidate you like. Otherwise, you can ruin your life and have the police watching you for a long time.

Y. We have talked about probation and deferred adjudication. Before we unleash you, let us mention one important thing about these matters: perform all of the requirements the judge orders for you to do during the probationary time. If you don't, the judge can order your arrest, bring you before him, revoke your probation, find you guilty, and impose the original punishment, like a fine and jail time. Just because you are on the street doesn't mean you can go wild. Use that opportunity to prove you have learned your lesson and are on the road to becoming a responsible citizen. This is important stuff; treat it like that.

During an interview for a radio station, the reporter asked a criminal judge to give his best advice to young people about the criminal law. The judge thought for only a moment before saying, "It is most important to avoid things and places that can lead you into trouble."

You need to know what those things and places are. Hopefully, this book has helped you do so. Everything you do has lasting consequences. Make yours good ones.

APPENDIX ONE

(Some Texas criminal laws and punishments)

CRIME	DESCRIPTION	PUNISHMENT
Capital Murder (Capital Felony)	Causing death during another felony or to a police officer or fireman in the course of his/her duties	Death or life imprisonment w/o parole
Murder (Felony First Degree)	Intentionally causing death of another person	Jail from 5 to 99 years and/or fine up to $10,000
Murder by Passion (Felony Second Degree)	Intentionally causing the death of another person brought about by passion	Jail from 2 to 20 years and/or fine up to $10,000*
Manslaughter (Felony Second Degree)	Recklessly causing the death of another person	Jail from 2 to 20 years and fine up to $10,000*
Criminally Negligent Homicide (State Jail Felony)	Negligently causing the death of another person	Jail from 180 days to 2 years and/or fine up to $10,000*
Unlawful Restraint (State Jail Felony)	Restraining a person's movement or liberty against his will	Jail from 180 days to 2 years and/or fine up to $10,000*
Kidnapping (Felony Third Degree)	Exercising unlawful possession and control over a person to the exclusion of his liberty or of persons having rightful possession and control of the person	Jail from 2 to 10 years and/or fine up to $10,000*
Aggravated Kidnapping (Felony First Degree)	Exercising unlawful possession and control over a person to the exclusion of his liberty or of persons having rightful possession and control of the person, for purposes of ransom or holding a hostage	Jail from 5 to 99 years and/or fine up to $10,000*
Public Lewdness	Publicly engaging in lewd acts, such as touching one's genitals	Jail up to 1 year and/or fine up to

(Class A Misdemeanor)		$4,000*
Indecent Exposure (Class B Misdemeanor)	Exposing genitals w/ illegal intent	Jail up to 180 days and/or fine up to $2,000*
Indecency w/ Child (Felony Second Degree)	Sexual contact w/ child with illegal intent	Jail from 2 to 20 years and/or fine up to $10,000*
Assault (Class A Misdemeanor)	Intentionally causing unwanted physical contact w/ another person w/ actual ability to do so	Jail up to 1 year and/or fine up to $4,000*
Assault of Public Servant (Felony Third Degree)	Intentionally causing unwanted physical contact w/ a public servant w/ actual ability to do so	Jail from 2 to 10 years and fine up to $10,000*
Sexual Assault (Felony Second Degree)	Intentionally causing unwanted sexual contact w/ another person w/ actual ability to do so	Jail from 2 to 20 years and/or fine up to $10,000*
Coercing Gang Membership (State Jail Felony)	Intentionally forcing a person to join a gang	Jail from 180 days to 2 years and/or fine up to $10,000*
Injury to Child, Elderly Person, Disabled Person (Felony First Degree)	Intentionally causing harm to a child, elderly person, or disabled person	Jail from 2 to 99 years and/or fine up to $10,000
Endangering Child (State Jail Felony)	Intentionally placing a child in a potentially harmful situation	Jail from 180 days to 2 years*
Terrorist Threat (Felony Third Degree)	Using threat of violence to impair communications, scare the public, interfere w/ government	Jail from 2 to 10 years and/or fine up to $10,000*
Tampering w/ Consumer	Altering a product intended for public use causing serious injury to a person	Jail from 5 to 99 years and/or fine

		up to $10,000
Product w/ Serious Injury (Felony First Degree)		up to $10,000
Leaving Child in Car (Class A Misdemeanor)	Intentionally leaving a child in a car for more than a brief time	Jail up to 1 year and/or fine up to $4,000*
Criminal Nonsupport (State Jail Felony)	Intentionally failing to discharge a legal obligation of support of a child	Jail from 180 days to 2 years and/or fine up to $10,000*
Arson of a Building (Felony Third Degree)	Intentionally causing a fire to a building	Jail from 2 to 10 years and/or fine up to $10,000*
Criminal Mischief- Damage from $500 to $1,500 (Class A Misdemeanor)	Intentionally causing damage to property of another person	Jail up to 1 year and/or fine up to $4,000*
Graffiti- Damage to $500 (Class B Misdemeanor)	Intentionally defacing property of another person	Jail up to 180 days and/or fine up to $2,000*
Aggravated Robbery (Felony Second Degree)	Theft of property with weapon or causing injury to another person	Jail from 2 to 20 years and/or fine up to $10,000*
Burglary of House (Felony Second Degree)	Intentionally and illegally entering another person's home w/ intent to remove property of another person	Jail from 2 to 20 years and/or fine up to $10,000*
Burglary of Coin Operated Machine or Burglary of Vehicle (Class A	Intentionally and illegally entering a vending machine or vehicle w/ intent to remove property of another person	Jail up to 1 year and/or fine up to $4,000*

Misdemeanor)		
Criminal Trespass (Class C Misdemeanor)	Intentionally entering the property of another person w/ knowledge of lack of authority	Fine up to $500*
Theft-Value $500 to $1,500 (Class A Misdemeanor)	Intentionally taking the property of another person	Jail up to 1 year and/or fine up to $4,000*
Unauthorized Use of Vehicle (State Jail Felony)	Intentionally exercising control and use of the vehicle of another person	Jail from 180 days to 2 years and/or fine up to $10,000*
Tampering w/ ID Number (Class A Misdemeanor)	Intentionally tampering with or altering the ID number of property	Jail up to 1 year and/or fine up to $4,000*
Theft of Video Services (Class C Misdemeanor)	Intentionally taking video or cable transmissions without paying for them	Fine up to $500*
Forgery (Felony Third Degree)	Falsely imitating the signature or facsimile authorization or electronic approval of another person	Jail from 2 to 10 years and/or fine up to $10,000*
Credit/Debit Card Abuse (State Jail Felony)	Using the credit or debit card of another person without permission and with the intent to confer an illegal gain on the user	Jail from 180 days to 2 years and/or fine up to $10,000*
Hindering Secured Creditor (Class A Misdemeanor)	Intentionally hindering a secured creditor in the lawful use of his security interest	Jail up to 1 year and/or fine up to $4,000*
Illegal Recruitment of Athlete-Value $1,500 to $20,000 (State Jail Felony)	Offering or receiving anything of value to influence a high school athlete in the selection of a college or university	Jail from 180 days to 2 years and/or fine up to $10,000*
Breach of Computer	Intentionally compromising the security of a computer or other	Jail up to 1 year and/or fine up to

Security-Value up to $1,500 (Class A Misdemeanor)	electronic device which stores information subject to being secured in the device	$4,000*
Perjury-Court (Felony Third Degree)	Intentionally falsifying testimony in court or in deposition intended to be used in court as testimony	Jail from 2 to 10 years and/or fine up to $10,000*
Failure to Identify (Class B Misdemeanor)	Intentionally failing to identify oneself to a peace officer when asked to do so	Jail up to 180 days and/or fine up to $2,000*
Resisting Arrest-No Weapon (Class A Misdemeanor)	Intentionally resisting the arrest of a peace officer, whether or not the underlying charge is valid	Jail up to 1 year and/or fine up to $4,000*
Evading Arrest (Class B Misdemeanor)	Intentionally evading a peace officer seeking to arrest the evader	Jail up to 180 days and/or fine up to $2,000*
Disorderly Conduct (Class C Misdemeanor)	Engaging in unruly or disturbing conduct that provokes a public disturbance	Fine up to $500*
False Report (Class A Misdemeanor)	Filing a false report with a government office	Jail up to 1 year and/or fine up to $4,000*
Harassment (Class B Misdemeanor)	Intentionally communicating with or about a person to embarrass, annoy, torment, harass that person	Jail up to 180 days and/or fine up to $2,000*
Stalking (Felony Third Degree)	Intentionally pursuing another person whereby he fears he may be physically harmed or killed	Jail from 2 to 10 years and/or fine up to $10,000*
Use of Laser (Class C Misdemeanor)	Intentionally pointing a laser at the eyes of another person	Fine up to $500*
Child Pornography-Possession (Felony Third Degree)	Intentionally possessing material depicting children under eighteen years of age engaging in sexual conduct	Jail from 2 to 10 years and/or fine up to $10,000*
Hoax Bomb (Class A Misdemeanor)	Intentionally pretending to possess or use a bomb to influence or alarm other persons	Jail up to 1 year and/or fine up to $4,000*

Gambling (Class C Misdemeanor)	Participating in an illegal gambling operation		Fine up to $500*
Public Intoxication (Class C Misdemeanor)	Being intoxicated in a public place		Fine up to $500*
DWI-First Offense (Class B Misdemeanor)	Driving while intoxicated-blood alcohol level .08+		Jail up to 180 days and/or fine up to $2,000 plus loss of driver's license*#
DRUG TYPE	**CRIMINAL ACTIVITY**	**CRIME**	**PUNISHMENT**
Controlled substance (heroine, cocaine, Meth-amphetamine, etc.)	Sale: 4+ to 200 g.	First Degree Felony	See above punishments for these crimes
	1 to 4 g.	Second Degree Felony	
	less than 1 g.	State Jail Felony	
	Possession: 200+ to 400 g.	First Degree Felony	
	4+ to 200 g.	Second Degree Felony	
	1 to 4 g.	Third Degree Felony	
	less than 1 g.	State Jail Felony	

Marijuana	Sale: 50+ lbs. to 2,000 lbs.	First Degree Felony	See above punishments for these crimes
	5+ to 50 lbs.	Second Degree Felony	
	¼ oz. to 5 lbs.	State Jail Felony	
	less than ¼ oz.	Class A Misdemeanor	
	Possession: 5+ lbs. to 50 lbs.	Third degree Felony	
	4+ oz. to 5 lbs.	State Jail Felony	
	2 to 4 oz.	Class A Misdemeanor	
	less than 2 oz.	Class B Misdemeanor	

*Each of these punishments can be increased if the defendant has prior criminal convictions or is a habitual offender. #DUI-First Offense is a Class C Misdemeanor, punished by: $500 fine, alcohol class, community service, loss of driver's license. Attempt to purchase alcohol or lying about age, by minor, is a class C Misdemeanor for the first offense, with similar punishment.

There is no probation for: DWI, intoxicated assault, intoxicated manslaughter, indecency w/ child, or sexual assault if the defendant previously had received community supervision for one of these crimes.

APPENDIX TWO

FEDERAL AGENCIES (Washington, DC):
Department of Labor (For Minimum Wage, Overtime, and Other Employment Law Matters)
866-487-2365
http://www.dol.gov

Occupational Safety and Health Administration (For Worker Safety Matters)
800-321-6742, 202-693-2000
http://www.osha.gov

Federal Citizen Information Center (For General Federal Law/Information Questions)
800-333-4636

Equal Employment Opportunity Commission (For Employment Discrimination Matters)
800-669-4000, 202-663-4900
http://www.eeoc.gov

FEDERAL AGENCIES (Regional Offices):

Department of Labor:

Atlanta: 404-302-3900	Kansas City: 816-285-1800
Boston: 617-565-9600	Los Angeles: 626-229-1000
Chicago: 312-353-0900	New York: 212-607-8600
Cincinnati: 859-578-4680	Philadelphia: 215-861-5300
Dallas: 972-850-4500	San Francisco: 415-625-2481

Occupational Safety and Health Administration:

Atlanta: 404-562-2300   Kansas City: 816-283-8745

Boston: 617-565-9860   New York: 212-337-2378

Chicago: 312-353-2220   Philadelphia: 215-861-4900

Denver: 720-264-6550   San Francisco: 800-475-4020

Dallas: 972-850-4145   Seattle: 206-553-5930

STATE WORKERS' RIGHTS AGENCIES (For Termination, Workers' Compensation, Safety, and Pay Matters):

Alabama Department of Labor (Montgomery) 334-242-3460
http://www.alalabor.state.al.us

Alaska Department of Labor (Juneau) 907-465-2700
http://www.labor.state.ak.us

Arizona Industrial Commission (Phoenix) 602-542-4515
http://www.ica.state.az.us

Arkansas Department of Labor (Little Rock) 501-682-4500
http://www.arkansas.gov/labor

California Department of Industrial Relations (San Francisco) 415-703-4810
http://www.dir.ca.gov/dlse

Colorado Department of Labor (Denver) 303-318-8441
http://www.coworkforce.com

Connecticut Department of Labor (Wethersfield) 860-263-6000
http://www.ctdol.state.ct.us

Delaware Department of Labor (Wilmington) 302-761-8200
http://www.delawareworks.com

District of Colombia Department of Employment (Washington, DC)
202-724-7000
http://does.dc.gov

Florida Department of Employment and Labor (Tallahassee) 850-
487-1395
http://www.stateofflorida.com/labem.html

Georgia Department of Labor (Atlanta) 404-232-3001, 877-709-8185
http://www.dol.state.ga.us

Hawaii Department of Labor (Honolulu) 808-586-8842
http://www.hawaii.gov/labor

Idaho Department of Labor (Boise) 208-332-3570
http://labor.idaho.gov

Illinois Department of Labor (Springfield) 800-645-5784, 217-782-
6206
http://www.state.il.us/agency/idol

Indiana Department of Labor (Indianapolis) 317-232-2655
http://www.in.gov/labor

Iowa Workforce Development Agency (Des Moines) 800-562-4692,
515-281-5387
http://www.iowaworkforce.org/labor

Kansas Department of Labor (Topeka) 785-296-5000
http://www.dol.ks.gov

Kentucky Department of Labor (Frankfort) 502-564-3070
http://labor.ky.gov

Louisiana Workforce Commission (Baton Rouge) 225-342-3111
http://www.laworks.net

Maine Department of Labor (Augusta) 207-623-7900
http://www.state.me.us/labor

Maryland Department of Labor (Baltimore) 410-230-6001
http://www.dllr.state.md.us

Massachusetts Department of Labor (Boston) 617-626-5400
http://www.mass.gov

Michigan Department of Labor (Lansing) 517-373-1820
http://www.michigan.gov/dleg

Minnesota Department of Labor (St. Paul) 800-342-5354, 651-284-5005
http://www.dli.mn.gov

Mississippi Department of Employment (Jackson) 601-321-6000
http://www.mdes.ms.gov

Missouri Department of Labor (Jefferson City) 573-751-3403
http://www.dolir.mo.gov

Montana Department of Labor (Helena) 406-444-2840
http://dli.mt.gov

Nebraska Department of Labor (Omaha) 402-595-3095
http://www.dol.state.ne.us

Nevada Department of Labor (Las Vegas) 702-486-2650
http://laborcommissioner.com

New Hampshire Department of Labor (Concord) 603-271-3176
http://www.labor.state.nh.us

New Jersey Department of Labor (Trenton) 609-777-3200
http://www.nj.gov/labor

New Mexico Department of Workforce (Albuquerque) 505-843-1900
http://www.dws.state.nm.us

New York Department of Labor (Albany) 888-469-7365, 518-457-9000
http://www.labor.state.ny.us

North Carolina Department of Labor (Raleigh) 800-625-2267, 919-807-2796
http://www.nclabor.com

North Dakota Department of Labor (Bismarck) 800-582-8032, 701-328-2660
http://www.nd.gov/labor

Ohio Department of Commerce (Reynoldsburg) 614-644-2450
http://www.com.ohio.gov/laws

Oklahoma Department of Labor (Oklahoma City) 888-269-5353, 405-521-6100
http://www.ok.gov/odol

Oregon Bureau of Labor (Portland) 971-673-0761
http://www.boli.state.or.us

Pennsylvania Department of Labor (Philadelphia) 215-560-1858
http://www.dli.state.pa.us

Rhode Island Department of Labor (Cranston) 401-462-8000
http://www.dlt.state.ri.us

South Carolina Department of Labor (Columbia) 803-896-4300
http://www.llr.state.sc.us

South Dakota Department of Labor (Pierre) 605-773-3681
http://dol.sd.gov

Tennessee Department of Labor (Nashville) 615-741-6642, 165-741-1627
http://www.tennessee.gov/labor-wfd

Texas Workforce Commission (Austin) 800-832-2829, 512-463-2222
http://www.twc.state.tx.us

Utah Labor Commission (Salt Lake City) 800-530-5090, 801-530-6800
http://www.laborcommission.utah.gov

Vermont Department of Labor (Montpelier) 802-828-4000
http://www.labor.vermont.gov

Virginia Department of Labor (Richmond) 804-371-2327
http://www.doli.virginia.gov

Washington Department of Labor (Tumwater) 800-547-8367, 866-219-7321
http://www.lni.wa.gov

West Virginia Division of Labor (Charleston) 304-558-7890
http://www.wvlabor.org

Wisconsin Department of Workforce (Milwaukee) 414-227-4384
http://www.dwd.state.wi.us

Wyoming Department of Employment (Cheyenne) 307-777-7261
http://wydoe.state.wy.us

If you call an agency, be persistent in locating the office for your specific problem. Explain your need and ask for help in locating someone who can assist you. If you get an uncooperative person, try again, but keep trying. Eventually, you will get to the right person.

INDEX